BRAND*VANTAGE*

ADVANCE PRAISE FOR THE BOOK

'I wish *Brandvantage* were around when I started my corporate journey decades ago! Arvind and Trupti, who punch in more than four decades of experience between them, have expertise in conceptualizing, creating, managing, nurturing, growing and curating some of the most iconic global and local brands. *Brandvantage* is a compendium of some of the most critical "hardware" and "software" every brand marketer, or indeed business person, needs. A must-read for every young marketer starting his or her starry-eyed journey to create a new brand icon or the seasoned one who takes a "pit stop" to refresh vital skill sets'—Suresh Narayanan, chairman and managing director, Nestlé India

'Learning is an ongoing process. Business schools start with the principles and learnings till the date of your course completion. Thereafter, one begins the journey of learnings from the experience of others combined with your own learnings. This book is a bridge between business school and your travels'—Piyush Pandey, chief creative officer, Ogilvy Worldwide and executive chairman, Ogilvy India

'*Brandvantage* is an easy-to-use guide that can help take your brand towards leadership in these hyper-competitive times. It very simply takes one through the process of brand building, from mining insights to targeting and developing communication to shaping a cult brand while staying agile and focused on the consumer. Real tips for today's marketers'—Lloyd Mathias, business strategist and senior marketer, HP Asia, Motorola and PepsiCo

'Trupti and Arvind are what I call serious knowledge compasses and serial authors and through their second joint book on the art and science of brand building called *Brandvantage*, they offer a new playbook through their own insights. As practitioners, they have first-hand knowledge of how to build brands and businesses with old brand fundamentals and new-age digital tools. I can say this book is a laser-guided missile of knowledge and a brand vitamin for business owners and brand builders. Read the book to get fresh ideas and contextual frameworks that work in the real-life digital economy'—Dr Annurag Batra, chairman and editor-in-chief, *BW Businessworld*

'A first-of-its-kind master guide which trains you on not just superlative brand management but also on elevating your leadership journey. A must-read for every aspiring and practising marketer'—Shital Mehta, managing director, Lifestyle International

'A masterpiece must quintessentially be simple. An amazing one for anyone who has been intrigued or challenged by building a brand. So intuitive, yet powerful. This book packs more than a punch'—Prabir Jha, founder and chief executive officer, Prabir Jha People Advisory

'*Brandvantage* lays out essential and holistic principles of brand management in a twelve-week journey, along with "office art" organizational enablers and career management skills to build cult brands and a sterling career. Grab it'—Deepika Warrier, chief marketing officer, Diageo India

'*Brandvantage* is a must-read for marketing and brand-building professionals, especially in their early professional years. The practical approach suggested by the authors is a testimony to the fact that both Trupti and Arvind have been practitioners of this art/science in their careers. The essence of brand management has been distilled and sharpened into a twelve-week journey to build formidable brands and one's career. Highly recommended'—Vipul Prakash, chief operating officer, MakeMyTrip, and ex-chief marketing officer, PepsiCo India

'A brilliant step-by-step guide for successful brand management and consumer engagement. What makes it real are the case studies and personal experiences from the brand masters themselves'—Vivek Sharma, chief marketing officer, Pidilite

A **12-WEEK** MASTER PLAN FOR
BRAND LEADERSHIP AND BEYOND

BRAND*VANTAGE*

TRUPTI BHANDARI
ARVIND BHANDARI

BUSINESS
An imprint of Penguin Random House

PENGUIN BUSINESS

USA | Canada | UK | Ireland | Australia
New Zealand | India | South Africa | China

Penguin Business is part of the Penguin Random House group of companies
whose addresses can be found at global.penguinrandomhouse.com

Published by Penguin Random House India Pvt. Ltd
4th Floor, Capital Tower 1, MG Road,
Gurugram 122 002, Haryana, India

First published in Penguin Business by Penguin Random House India 2021

10 9 8 7 6 5 4 3 2 1

ISBN 9780670095315

Typeset in Adobe Garamond Pro by Manipal Technologies Limited, Manipal
Printed at Replika Press Pvt. Ltd, India

www.penguin.co.in

To our parents, Suresh and Shama Narvekar,
and Balbir Singh and Kanchan Bhandari

Contents

Introduction   xi

Week 1: Know the Business, the Brand and the Manager   1

Week 2: Deep Dive into Your Brand   17

Week 3 and 4: What Does the Consumer Need?   43

Week 5 and 6: How Do I Diagnose a Problem?   59

Week 7 and 8: Know Your Consumer   74

Week 9: How Do I Segment and Target Him/Her?   98

Week 10: How Do I Position My Brand?   117

Week 11 and 12: How Do I Communicate with Her?   146

The Next Three Months: Can I Shape a Cult Brand?   173

Second-last Quarter: How Do I Surround My Consumer?   200

Final Quarter: Where, Why, When Do I Innovate?   220

Last Tip: Behaving like Start-ups   239

Epilogue   251
Bibliography   257

Introduction

In our professional lives, spanning almost five decades in building some of India's most formidable brands, we have seen managers either walk to glory or sink into oblivion or pitiable mediocrity. Likewise, we have seen brands grow or stagnate with a strong correlation to the performance of managers who were tasked with handling these brands. When we looked closer, we found an underlying pattern amongst a host of factors, which determines success or failure.

Brandvantage is dedicated to uncovering these enabling factors that lead to both personal and professional growth, hitherto not understood in this way where personality attributes and professional results interact with each other to make a difference.

Intuitively, all of us focus on what it takes to be a competent professional. That leads us to the search of superlative knowledge, processes and tools to pave the way for success. Occasionally, we even turn to peers and seniors to learn by asking, but for the most part, our growth is circumscribed by an approach of acquiring functional competencies so our performance speaks for us.

When we looked at high performers, we realized that the success of the brand is invariably associated with the success of the brand manager. A great idea cannot be delivered in an uninspiring, stuttering speech, and a great brand cannot be built if its purveyor is not a successful brand manager. And this is not a chicken-and-egg sequential dilemma of what comes first: the successful brand or the brand manager, but a reflection of the reality that the two grow in tandem, feeding off each other. The two, the brand manager and the brand, are inextricably linked and we fail to acknowledge them because they are connected to a host of factors that are either not understood; or perceived to be not easy to link and leverage successfully. Exploring further, we found that the success of a brand and a brand manager is in turn determined by things that may often be accidental; but hearteningly, if we recognize them, these factors needn't be left to chance to benefit us.

Narrowing it down, we mined three factors that work as a hidden cause to aid functional competencies. If you have the luck of the draw, these will catapult you to success, and if they are missing, they will undermine you at every step of your professional growth. You just cannot afford to let these factors not come to assist you. What are they?

Managers of all types are assisted by the holy concurrence of:

- The timing and completeness of their initial learning curve. Put simply, managers have to learn critical things in the initial few weeks and learn them reasonably comprehensively to connect the dots and make a difference to stand out in the competitive clutter.
- The ability to understand the stage of the business that their brand is at and to make the right strategic moves. All too often, most managers plunge into the warfare with same weapons and same intensity, without estimating the diverse landscape of the competitive wars. Appreciating this allows them to build early cross-alliances and anticipate future moves for growing themselves and their brands simultaneously.
- Finally, assessing their soft skills in the context of the business situation and leveraging their strengths, and supplementing

their weaknesses constantly without trying everything and losing energy and initial enthusiasm. This goes a long way in building their credibility to help them succeed with their brand initiatives.

Brandvantage has been written to make these fortuitous factors work for you. The effect of these in making your initial endeavours matter is not different from the extra push that a swimmer feels when cruising in the direction of the stream. Without its additional benefits, the difficulty for the unfortunate swimmer is obvious and we hope you are not amongst those deprived of the gentle nudge of favourable forces.

Through the book, we will chaperon you in the first twelve weeks of brand and self-management, so that hidden factors come into play and build your confidence for growing your credibility, which is so essential for the success of the brand. Embedded with familiar and new frameworks, you will find insightful examples in the book that will help you get on board fast. Confounding information is sifted through for getting an initial advantage and building rapid competencies to lead the brand to growth.

After the twelve weeks, as your growth acquires a certain momentum, you will be ready to face the world—to craft your cult brands and sally beyond.

The book has been structured to make tough learning a natural process. We have mixed qualitative and quantitative aspects of business, excel-drilling and experiential learning, desk-research and people-learning to make growth joyful, and lead you towards an effortless discovery of new business wins.

Who will it benefit? Managers who want to lead their business to success by tapping the font of growth: 'consumer value' bundled in the offering of a brand. Whether you have just taken on a brand, or wish to excel midway through your career, or refashion your personal and brand journey for more impact, this book will assist you in building formidable business acumen.

In sum, *Brandvantage* will help you build the brand even as it helps you build the carrier of the brand: you.

So let's get into your shoes to get started.

Week 1

Know the Business, the Brand and the Manager

As a brand custodian, the future of business will follow your footsteps. Whether you trekked through arduous days in sales to earn your brand stint, or your marketing talent was spotted by an influential senior, or you were plain lucky . . . whatever the trajectory, you are now looking ahead at two possibilities. Either you will catapult the brand to dizzy heights or consign it to oblivion. Brand management is fraught with consequences and you have the pivotal role to create a legacy or none at all.

Yes, nowhere is the impact of an individual on business so apparent and so directly correlatable, as in brand management. That makes brand management a very coveted position. So where do we start? With your BQ?

BQ: Brand Quotient

What's your BQ or Brand Quotient? IQ or Intelligence Quotient and EQ or Emotional Quotient are common currency these days, signifying inherent mental acuity and emotional control in individuals which determine their chances of success. The higher the score, the better. We are coining BQ or brand quotient as a determinant of success which comprises:

- The hard **brand competencies** that you must know, almost like the hardware. These are the essential functional tools that you must have the whole box of.
- The whole gamut of **managerial skills** that you need to have or bring to bear on your brand management. It's the software complement to the above.
- The **office art,** the fuzzy stuff that is hard to recognize, even more difficult to develop and seldom spoken of, but has a strong impact on the success of your brand as well as your career. It connects the hardware of brand competencies and the software of managerial skills, creating the right environment for you and your brand to succeed.

Figure 1.1: BQ elements

In our experience, the three are intertwined. Those who do well happen to have—through a fortuitous concurrence of talent, coaching, guidance and hard work—a high representation of most of these traits. Those who do poorly show a marked deficit on most of these. Through this book, we will help maximize the success of those who are doing well, as much as lead the underperformers out of the pit they find themselves in. Let's understand these in detail to know how we can develop our BQ as we go through this book.

Brand competencies

On campus, students pick up a lot of academic information on running brands. In our experience, managers are unable to apply their learnings when they shift from the book to the hustle and bustle of real life. The quiet unchallenged world of paradigms on pieces of paper just seems to fly out of their minds, as bosses under the weight of the real world descend on them. Also, a manager typically takes a few years before he makes it to brand management and the intervening gap between learning and application is too long for one's memory to be of much help. The result in either case is a rather clueless employee waiting for some direction from a line manager who may or may not be able to help. And if the business situation is not very challenging, you can miss the learning opportunity altogether in the initial years..

In reality, the brand questions are rather intuitive and, if followed with earnestness and some guidance, they can be resolved to grow business. But that doesn't happen usually because managers struggling with disparate pieces of information embedded in obscure corporate jargon, fail to join the dots and diagnose a problem correctly to develop appropriate solutions.

In BQ, we have approached business subjects in a natural inquisitive way so that the academic learnings of MBA effortlessly weave into problem analysis and solution, without seeming burdensome. For example, when you want to address a person's health, you make inquiries about him, identify his type, understand his need and reference him to similar people to understand what to address. Then, you communicate with him the changes you want to bring about, give him new solutions and try to cover all his areas of interaction to enable him to move towards exceptional health and well-being.

In a similar spirit, we have approached brand competencies from the following perspectives to evaluate a problem or opportunity holistically and deliver solutions comprehensively, covering in brief:

- Who is my consumer? (Where, Why, When, What . . .)
- What does he need? (fundamentals of marketing)
- How do I segment and target him?
- How do I position my brand?
- How do I communicate with her?
- How do I surround her? (integrated marketing)
- How, when, why do I innovate?
- How do I make a brand that consumers love? (cult brand)

All these have been developed in a linear way, timed over the next one year, with a steep learning curve in the first twelve weeks to give you a head start.

It is our belief that if you understand and apply all or most of these fundamental tools, you will kick-start your career and give your brand a chance to shine in a way that no good fortune or customized training can do for you.

Business types and corresponding managerial skills

But for any journey to end well, it's important that we know what we have in stock. In this case, the biggest stock is you—rather, us as individuals. So, we will first look at ourselves to know who we truly are as managers. That way we will know what we need to capitalize on and where we need to improve or even supplement our capabilities by enlisting the help of other people. Success then becomes predictable, not accidental. But different managerial skills come into play depending on the business situation. Therefore, to understand yourself, let's look at businesses from a bird's-eye view.

All businesses don't have the same purpose. By reason of their stage of evolution or what is expected of them, they have a different outlook. The brands you work on are bound to be impacted by the framework of business within which they operate. It's important that you appreciate the business situation to make better brand choices. Businesses will typically fall into one of these types:

Turnaround: We hear this often because there is a bit of drama around it. Businesses that are registering less growth with a sense of impending crisis. The need for a vision, visionary and bold moves . . . Most people want to participate in this situation if the prospect of emerging successful is high, since it offers gallantry awards for business warriors at the end. This situation requires leaders with vision, working with a sense of urgency, leading a team with well-articulated purpose. Brands in this situation need to be repurposed, recommunicated, renovated or innovated. Brand managers who prefer these things succeed well in this environment.

Maintenance: The opposite of the above. Business is doing well; systems, strategy, technology, structures are chiming in happy unison and growth is an easy derivative. What is the role of the managers? Well, keep the clock ticking nicely, lubricate what is running slow, and proactively look for factors that could spoil the party to pre-empt or eliminate them altogether before any threat to business continuity shows up.

Managers of such firms need to be steadfast and disciplined. They need to keep reviewing processes routinely to not let complacency lay seeds of rot. They have to maintain a tight watch on people's morale while challenging them consistently in the absence of a clear threat. They should be looking for efficiencies and incremental gains in a well-optimized system so that success is not taken for granted. Brand managers of this eco-system have to maximize what's working, not fix what isn't broken. They have to build loyalty, develop engagement programmes with consumers and ward off competition with the forbidding intensity of a predator that is typical of a market leader.

Turnaround and Maintenance are two opposite ends and if the manager who excels in one is mistakenly put in the other situation, disaster is almost certain.

Expanding: In this situation, the business has had a good start with a strong consumer franchise, albeit small. Investment is waiting to follow strategy as more growth is only a matter of time. Typically, in a case of expanding, the category is either being re-shaped by a disruptive idea that challenges the status quo—like the emergence of Oyo Rooms and Airbnb as low cost, clean alternatives to big hotels—or a whole new alternative is being set up as a counter to prevalent technology such as the electric cars of Tesla against the fossil fuel-driven cars, making the old technology appear dated. In essence, the business here is looking for escape velocity to gain scale rapidly and become attractive to investors and adopters alike.

Managers required here are a mix of specialists and generalists. Those who operate on specific parts of the business with the ability to multiply by debottlenecking: procurement, logistics, finance, marketing. High competence, big on energy, able to work in large teams loosely structured, and driven by a shared vision. Small companies with clear funding and strategic direction fit in this space, like the multinationals in early years. They attract talent and bring out the best in brand practices, being open to experimenting-executing-learning-launching-relearning. Pepsi, ICICI Bank, Frito-Lay, Dabur

Foods—these companies exhibited such traits and gobbled up the best brand managerial talent with opportunities to grow, for the business and people alike.

Reinventing: These are companies in no particular trouble, at least as yet, but argue for a re-alignment of their strategy, structures and processes to stay relevant and win in the next decade or so. A part of their business may be ailing and needs to be hived off or reconfigured, or a certain outside factor is asking for a retooling, such as updating IT systems for a paint company like Asian Paints, or a new culture needs to be brought in to mould out of the current archaic one. Managers in this situation need to have a clear agenda, and the ability to rally people around a goal. They need to disrupt without causing pain and manage business continuity without any breaks. In other words, they need to reinvent the business so that a constant growth rate is delivered in the present and future. But they have to do all this while the business is running, since they don't have the luxury of stopping to restart. In other words, they have to refuel mid-air.

Brand managers of this work environment need to change what needs to be changed, while reinforcing what's working with great prudence and discretion. Consumers at the far end of this momentous journey should see no discontinuity in the services arising from internal alignment, continuing to be delighted as before. It's a rare 'stop-start' skill that requires as much innovativeness as it does compliance.

Start-up: If in scaling up, the manager knows the road ahead and all she needs to do is to gallop faster, start-up is about choosing the best road among the many amorphous ones unfolding ahead. The guiding beacon in this maze of uncertainty is any opportunity that is crying to be served, and the modus operandi is literally anything that makes it happen fast. Funds are erratic, business processes are unfounded, teams are still being put together, and the only clarity in this fuzzy situation is that you need to act fast, almost running as you learn to walk—before competitors overtake you.

Managers of this situation love and thrive on ambiguity as their zeal drives them to create the road to the realized goal. Lack of formalism, unbounded energy, strong functional knowledge, high team-building capabilities and an insatiable appetite to get to that elusive first billion are their core qualities. Brand managers in this situation need to be high on creativity, resilience, functional skills and doughty enough to navigate the open seas of uncertainty.

So which business do you fit into? If you are beginning to get some sense of where your business is slotted, the next question to ask is, 'Am I up to it?' We dwelt at length to typecast about a hundred-plus managers we have coached, refined, rejected or enabled to paths of glory and found them falling in the archetypes that follow. Here is a mirror being offered to self-gaze and reflect upon oneself.

Managerial skills : STRIVES framework

In his book *What Is History,* E.H. Carr cautions the student of history to invest some time in knowing the historian. Likewise, before you go on to shape the brand, be aware of who you are as a person. After all, what you bring to bear on the brand, in our observation, has a strong correlation with who you are, as a person. What drives you, what repulses you, what you seek, what riles you up . . . Just as art is the expression of the artist, the brand is the brainchild and heartchild (the word doesn't exist, but why not?) of a brand manager.

This is the problem and the opportunity. Unlike art, brands are not owned by individuals, they are the heritage of companies. But as art aficionados know, knockout work comes when the artist is immersed in his creation. In the following pages, our attempt is to get the passion of an artist to brand management along with the cerebral discretion of the manager. So that what we get in the end is the best of art and commerce to bear on the brand.

Let's find the internal you as you spot yourself in one of the following self-portraits: Shaper (S), Team worker (T), Researcher (R), Improviser (I), Visionary (V), Executor (E), Specialist (S)—the STRIVES framework of managerial skills.

Shaper: You don't have any special skill but what general skill do you not have? You can understand anything in no time and find the quickest solution around it. You have unlimited contacts and you can bring them to bear on your work instinctively. If you are blocked one way, you can wriggle out in a million other ways. If a vision is given and a rough framework is in sight, you can shape the steps from the beginning to the end with ease. You make flow charts and process maps naturally, exude energy indefatigably, and realize the final result inexplicably. No project is complete without you because only you have the knowledge and capability to convert problems into enablers towards the end goal.

Team worker: Many think that you are their closest, exclusive ally, although in reality, the whole team is close to you. You are to organizations what a lubricant is to the engine—you slip in anywhere, becoming the social facilitator for keeping teams singing like one choir. You think people, solve problems with people, celebrate and lose with people. To you the world acquires meaning only in the context of people. This inordinate interest in people gives you a natural flair for understanding them: what glues them, what makes them drift; you sense it all and you use it to put motley teams together. You need others to define and justify you—as teams grow in size, so does your power, and your indispensability.

Researcher: Your reason to exist is to know. If there is a question, there has to be an answer however far it's hidden from view. You go deep into history, you scan laterally for current trends, you connect with insiders and outsiders of industry to figure out your way, you organize groups and test hypotheses. In less time than people take to understand the issue, you have analysed it threadbare in every possible way—qualitatively, quantitively, factually and intuitively. Now the information is ready to be acted upon and you step back for the next quiz. Action doesn't move you much and you let someone else take charge of what needs to follow knowledge, preferring to slay ignorance that comes in the way of knowing. You cannot see a task from one end to the other, but boy, you can empower the team with the knowledge to do so.

Improviser: You are not the first one to hit the new idea and when you are done, people may have difficulty attributing anything specific to you, but nobody can improve like you do. You can go to the last detail, the number at the bottom of the Excel sheet or an unrealized assumption, and look for savings and improvements where nobody suspected any. It's not just once, but you can keep unravelling processes and tools in the relentless pursuit of improvement, till the last drop of opportunity has been sucked out. You thrive on detail, have an eye to aggregate everyday minutiae to significant somethings, and you prosper in scarcity. In sum, you can bring magic with your hawk-like gaze for continuous improvement and the tenacity to work on it. Without you, there is no process optimization or cost minimization; you are a boon to those seeking improvement on ROI or return on investment.

Visionary: If you like to envision a new future, come up with new ideas that didn't exist before, and leave a legacy, you are wired to be an innovator. You have all the enthusiasm to rally resources behind a new, big cause, but you falter when it comes to details. You are also not the one who communicates very effectively in your pursuit of that elusive goal and you have little patience for elaborate processes since they seem to stonewall progress rather than aid it.

Without you, disruption would be a dream and the world would be fated to live in unending sameness. You are seminal to forward propulsion of business entities towards building competitiveness in the future.

Executor: If the goal is given and timelines defined, you swoop in effortlessly with intervening steps to achievement. You set up milestones, allocate responsibility, distribute resources and review to reward or punish, but you never fail to deliver. You are a god of reliability for your seniors and your execution skills are as certain as the axe of, well . . . the executor. You eliminate uncertainty with your mere appearance and guide people to the destination. The only problem is you can't strategize or decide on what's the best course of action in a given situation. But once someone has done that for you, they can step back and enjoy the results. You are a finisher without an exception. You will take all the painstaking effort and compromise the means (that could be a downside if not adequately overseen), but never the sacrosanct end.

Specialist: Generalities are of as much interest to you as grass is to a tiger. For you, the god is in the detail of the subject matter. It is there that truth is grasped, and in its absence, all is hogwash. You prefer to dig into your hole with a microscope, under reams of academic knowledge, burning the proverbial midnight oil and not emerging until you have the answer with the truth. When you talk, others shut up. You are the voice of specialized knowledge that no one dares contest, knowing the hardships leading up to your mastery of the subject. In a team, your perspective is priceless when all pivots around knowing the situation in detail and finality. The only problem: you have no interest in teams, action, final result. That is not the really joyous part of the rainbow as far as you are concerned.

So you have business types and you have corresponding managerial skills. How do they intersect? Can you be the right person at the right time, so results follow effortlessly? If not, can you manoeuvre the situation to your advantage? Let's cross tab the two situations and see what the perfect fitment is and where the synergy is low so that it can be improvised. The number of Y (Yes) indicates the strength of the fitment—the more there are, the better the fitment. N means none.

Figure 1.2: Business types and managerial skills cross tab

Business types/ managerial skills	Turnaround	Maintenance	Expanding	Re-inventing	Start-up
Shaper	YY	N	Y	YY	YYY
Team worker	YY	Y	YY	YY	YYY
Researcher	YY	Y	YY	Y	N
Improviser	Y	YY	YYYY	YY	N
Visionary	Y Y Y Y	N	YY	YY	YYY
Executor	Y	YYYY	YY	YY	Y
Specialist	Y	N	Y	YY	Y

You could debate some of the fitments above; there is no perfect answer, but some trends emerge. Visionaries are perfect for Turnaround and Start-ups, Improvisers for Expanding, Executors for Maintenance, Researchers and Specialists seem to fit in most places due to their exclusive contribution. Shapers and Team workers are important in most situations especially in Start-ups, Reinventing or Turnaround situations. So, there is hope for all manager archetypes since various business situations abound in the market for you to excel.

In the following chapters, as we acquire the competencies for brand management, we will also simultaneously learn how to be more suitable for the situation by either:

- Playing to our strengths, or
- Covering our weakness through enlisting the help of others to supplement us

This is based on the reality that no one person can possibly excel in all traits. But by being aware of the situation at hand, as well as our strengths, we can maximize our chances to succeed.

Office art

So, in addition to managerial skills of 'STRIVES' and brand competencies that we will explore at length, we will also develop office art, the environment where skills and competencies interact. These pertain to the fuzzy aspects of business that are difficult to articulate or template and hence, often not spoken of. But these can make all the difference between a spectacular success or a timid show. If brand competencies is the hardware of running the brand and managerial skill is the software, then office art is the creation of the fertile environment for competencies and skills to play out favourably.

What are these subtle things that constitute office art?

How to manage our boss and understand our company culture to maximize chances to succeed. How to strike cross alliances in the company to help our projects. Equally important are things which have a direct impact on our performance or the perception of it. Hence, we need to make an early impact in our job to build trust and confidence among the people around us. Going further, we will evaluate how to manage our time as also our team's, while being conscious of our inherent bias and prejudices to circumvent this.

We will cover this subtle office art, which is fluid and ever-evolving, in the first twelve weeks at the right points of time to impact your career favourably and establish your credibility as a manager. Inevitably, this will add to your confidence and help you push your agenda as a brand manager.

First twelve weeks and beyond

Before we take measured but quick plunges, a word about the criticality of time in the development of one's brand career. The reasons are founded on some empirical observations on how managers' initial moves determine their long-term careers.

Some managers show what is called the 'action imperative', meaning a tendency to move into action to demonstrate their impact, before figuring out the best alternatives for the situation. The result is either short-lived success or downright failure, leading to wastage.

Others sink into 'analysis paralysis', overwhelmed by the deluge of information to be considered or just the fear of untoward consequences of their actions. The result is long-drawn-out strategic presentations that define the problem but defy a solution. And managers who are brought to make positive change get knotted up in perpetual analysis, becoming a victim of their own hard work.

Finally, there are those who are unable to analyse or execute and so end up taking steps that are either least controversial, or popular or upheld by dominant and vocal managers, but which aren't usually good for the business or brand. Gradually such people lose their individuality as managers, missing an opportunity to sharpen their skills as political correctness becomes their natural style. For such managers, a crisis is waiting around the corner as they lack the competence to run a business.

Usually, the above inadequate reaction from managers appears because of their inability to leverage the first few weeks when the learning curve is steep, the company's acceptability of their mistakes is high and their ability to learn with sincerity is the maximum. If they perform well, they grow; if they miss, they still grow because learning still follows. A year down the line expectations mount and forbearance of mistakes is low. If managers haven't learnt in the critical learning period, they are destined to drive without adequate driving skills.

Further, if the start is shaky, the subsequent build-up is even more suspect. If the situation unfolds in a way that is different from the way you have been trained, you have little to fall back on since you lack the experience to handle complex unforeseen scenarios. As a result, business becomes vulnerable to competitions' attacks or worse still, consumer indifference, and a brand manager's career starts to head south.

The lack of structured on-boarding or hands-on learning in the first few months creates a failure that is misattributed to a lack of talent or competence of the manager. A manager's years of professional education and experience turns turtle when reality confronts—a situation that could have been averted if the initial period of brand management was chaperoned by trained hands. Given this reality, we intend to make a substantial difference in the initial period of a brand manager's career when the opportunity to learn and succeed is the highest.

The book is structured in two parts. The first twelve weeks of laying the foundation and the following nine months for building a formidable brand and a career. In twelve weeks, you would be ahead of your peers; in one year, you may be stretching towards unprecedented brand performance. To know the difference, please check your BQ now and do it after reading this book and following it up over the years.

Below is the summary of what skills and competencies you need to exhibit. Mark yourself on a score of 0 to 10. You may not be sure in all the cases but still go ahead and score yourself. Total the scores for each attribute and get the grand total of all the three totals. Your score on 230 (23 attributes multiplied by a maximum score of 10 each, like IQ) will tell you where you stand as of now.

We will revisit this at the end of the book and see the progress on these critical BQ parameters, as also your total BQ score.

Figure 1.3: BQ score grid

Managerial skills	Score (0-10)	Office art	Score (0-10)	Brand competencies	Score (0-10)
Shaper		Boss management		Brand knowledge	
Team worker		Making an early impact		Consumer need	
Researcher		Understanding company culture		Knowing the consumer	
Improviser		Effective cross-alliances		Segmentation and targeting	
Visionary		Checking tendency bias		Positioning	
Executor		Building team		Communication	
Specialist		Managing yourself		Cult brand	
				Integrated marketing	
				Innovation	
Total					
Grand Total					

Having glimpsed the landscape of the learning to follow, let's now take a plunge into the daunting but very rewarding world of brand management.

Week 2

Deep Dive into Your Brand

After the self-awareness session and identifying the stage of your company in the first week, you already have a head start. You know that all companies and brands are not at the same stage of development. You know that the real world is multi-faceted and a single monolithic stereotype idea of success is a myth. This understanding puts you ahead of your peers. You are equipped to identify the situation and tailor your response accordingly. Now let's get to work.

Managerial skill: Researcher

The office tends to suck people into routine firefighting and managers can easily lose their academic grounding. The ability to analyse a situation like reading a book is what sets managers apart from just workers in the company. It's important, therefore, that you retain your studying intensity at work to inform your decisions better at all times.

In the STRIVES framework, we would emphasize that you build the researcher aspect of your managerial skill early on to get good knowledge of your brand and what impacts it, with the discipline of an MBA course. Where you are unable to get the information to build on your knowledge, make sure you get someone else to help you, or put in place a system where you are able to get information at will and start to process it. After all, right knowledge precedes everything; most of all, right action, which your life is soon going to be full of.

What are the essential traits of a researcher and how can you encourage or inculcate this trait in yourself? A researcher's essential trait is the ability to organize a disorganized, unknown universe into a predictable landscape where he or she can be ready for any eventuality. Hence, as you plough through the second week at work, develop the following skills of a researcher.

- *Draw boundaries*: Understand in a very broad way what you need to know early on. This way, you will not get deluged by information; instead you will pick up the basics to start joining the dots to get the full picture. Just as before exploring a touristy town, you make a checklist of what vantage points you must cover in the limited time you have so that you are able to maximize viewing pleasure, similarly, lay out all that you need to know by identifying broad buckets of information pertaining to the brand (brand strategy, P&L, suppliers, demand, history . . .) and step back and see it from a distance to appreciate how much you have to learn. Of course, keep a count of time to do this with sustained interest.
- *Sequence search:* You may be overwhelmed by how much you need to know, so it's important to sequence things to structure up the learning. Ones closer to your immediate brand work should be taken first, followed by expanding spirals of the brand's interaction with other elements like raw material sourcing, stakeholder involvement, etc. It is also important to differentiate what's urgent and what you can influence on a day-to-day basis versus what's important but your immediate impact may be relatively low.
- *Take stock:* Occasionally see how robust your data is. Are you going too shallow to draw meaningful inferences or are you diving too deep in one aspect, losing the big picture and your

stamina to keep exploring? As you become more senior, you have
to develop an intuitive sense of how far to dig and where to let go.

- *Check truth and relevance:* With your newly acquired knowledge,
check now and then the veracity of your data as also its relevance.
It's easy to get lost in reams of academia but good researchers
enhance their contribution by being relevant. Develop the knack
to see if information is actionable or a mere mind-tickler. Ask
yourself if this is contemporary or is it dated. Assure yourself
that it enables you to look beyond the obvious and enriches your
perspective. Once you develop the discretion to differentiate, be
ruthless to abandon what doesn't work and sharpen what does.
A good manager excels at labouring where it matters, as much
as not labouring where it doesn't. Developing this skill early
minimizes mistakes later when the stakes are higher.

Being conscious of the above steps and implementing them often,
you can acquire the strengths of a researcher, which will stand you in
good stead in the long term. With the managerial skill of a researcher,
it's time now to start building the brand competence.

Brand: its anatomy

What is a brand? There are many ways the meaning implicit in the
word 'brand' can be unpacked. In the most clinical-sterile way, it's
a type of product manufactured by a particular company compliant
with a particular law. Meaning, it is a product or service with an
identifiable description and address, unlike nondescript, non-
traceable items that have no distinctive features, usually available
without a packaging. Let's start with the fundamentals of a brand.

Specificity is the first ingredient of a brand. It means they are
determinate and tangible in many ways: shape, texture, weight, smell,
touch, feel, sight: all the things that pertain to the senses. Existing in
various combinations, these physical manifestations set them apart

from others, imparting them with uniqueness. The more specific a brand's physical manifestations, the easier its recollection ahead of other brands. As physical manifestations develop, then just a mere symbol of the brand will enable consumers to recall the whole brand with just a glance. Think about McDonald's golden arches and the hunger-satisfying promise it signals from miles away, and you will understand the power of a single specific symbol to cue the whole experience.

Specificity is followed by **desirability**. There is no point in finding a brand and being dismayed by its undermining quality. Think of a food that is insipid, a cream that dries your skin, a disinfectant that increases vulnerability and a social media platform that makes you a sociopath—and you gather the significance of brands in enhancing one's lives. Desirability when well met leads to trust and respect. This makes the aspect of being wanted a critical feature of the brand.

Brands are **need-satisfiers** at the core. They fulfil a fundamental consumer need: physiological, social, self-esteem or higher order benefit of self-actualization. Stronger brands index higher on satisfying the needs of consumers better than weaker ones. The brand starts to peak when it becomes synonymous with a core need relevant to a category. Like Dettol for disinfecting, Xerox for photocopying, Fevicol for sticking things. However, as the market segments into many offerings from competing players, strong brands have to strengthen their benefit to satisfy the core need without any gap, to prevent other brands from walking in.

Brands have a **personality**, much like people. This gives them better relatability to their consumers and endears them to their patrons as favourites, friends, fans, or passionate followers. This may seem odd at first, but brands that lack facets of a living being stand a serious risk of being eroded by one that does. As we shall explore going ahead, true brand loyalty only starts when consumers relate to brands like they relate to real people. Having attributes that evoke human emotions helps brands become closer and dependable.

As brands grow, they also acquire a **heritage**, which is a summation of experiences built around repetitive and successful interactions between the consumers and the brands. The brand has a history of its origin, the evolution of its product and service offerings, and consumer experiences intertwined with their personal lives. For instance, the brand Maggi has a history of its packs, flavours and communication which many consumers recall. But that's not all. Consumers, independent of the company's communication, associate the brand intimately with their own lives. For some, it's a comfort food, for others it's closely associated with a passage of life, like moving from hostel life to working life to early married years. For some, it's a culinary delight beyond compare. When you add up all these billions of consumer experiences, you end up with the collective history of Maggi (which was a part of Maggi's campaign called 'Me and Meri Maggi' signifying consumers' unique endearing experiences with the brand) that constitutes a formidable heritage.

When brand managers invoke the heritage of brands, they deepen consumer trust, enriching it with strong emotions. Think of Apple, Maggi, Fabindia, Natural's ice cream, and you are inundated with images of your life experiences intertwined with the product. Nostalgia, hope, exhilaration, companionship: various emotions are suffused in brands with a deep heritage.

Not all brands have one; fewer still aspire to. But those brands that have a **world-view** stand taller and ahead of others. Having a world-view means not merely selling a product or a service, but standing for a value that surpasses mere physical-need satisfaction. It represents a brand's view about life at large when the brand interacts with society and therefore is beyond the mere expression of a product or service benefit that brands are normally equated with.

If the brand's world-view is well defined and expressed, then its loyalists will not only know and predict the brand's perspective, but they will also expect the brand to express it. Thus, having a world-view is rare and comes with great expectations from consumers, but if handled well, it results in loyalty beyond reason for the brand. For instance, Tata Tea stands not merely for its functional role of stimulation but also for 'awakening' in the figurative sense. It stands for creating awareness around issues that concern the betterment of society. Idea Cellular Network stands for ingenuity in life's trammels, from small to big issues, in keeping with its brand name. Nike has a world-view that upholds doing, however difficult or uncertain, over merely mulling over things, typified in its brand tagline 'Just do it'.

Furthermore, brands with a world-view increase their relevance to consumers and invite those who echo its interpretation of the world. If the world-view is well chosen and stoutly defended, its ability to win consumers can be phenomenal.

Finally, brands have a **philosophy**. While world-view represents its expanded view looking out at the world that it's a part of, philosophy is the inside look at itself—the inner core from which the brand draws its justification and sustenance. It's based on a fundamental human craving that has been assiduously unravelled by the brand, which it is fully committed towards satisfying. The brand in its everyday representation—its products and services—may occasionally get dated, but if its philosophy is well articulated then not only does it outlast a downturn but it can even surprise consumers with a proposition that is ahead of its time, with an understanding of the market that beats competitors. Most brands may not be able to articulate their philosophy, but the few who do insure their future from the vagaries of business.

Nike has the philosophy 'If you have a body, you are an athlete', expressed in its founder Bill Bowerman's idea. Google believes in the right of humans to have information available at a click. Walmart believes in making people save money so they can live better. The philosophical compass of these companies are visible in the vision of the companies or sometimes in the pronouncements of their founding fathers. Philosophy is an abstraction which may not be fully actualized but provides direction and fuel for growth in future.

In the final analysis, therefore, a brand is not only its physical representation but is as abstract as an idea. If you have an idea that is pivoted on fulfilling a fundamental consumer need with a unique solution, consistently and assiduously, you have a brand. If not, you have a mere product, a commodity that is continuously threatened by indistinguishable me-too's.

How does your brand score on the attributes mentioned above? Give your brand a score from 0 to 10 on the following assessment and test its strength. We insist you do this first because if a brand is well known, then you must be able to pick its distinctive features even before you have become its champion. It's a good time to score your brand because you are as good as a consumer right now. When you have finished your brand stint, you can come back and assess your brand on the same attributes and see if you have made a difference.

Figure 2.1: Brand strength assessment

Brand Attribute	Score 0 to 10 (low to high)
Specificity	
Desirability	
Need-satisfaction	
Personality	
Heritage	
World-view	
Philosophy	

Once you get the total score of these attributes, your brand is one of the following.

0 to 20	Weakling
20 to 40	Aspiring
40 to 60	Formidable
Above 60	Cult

Now that you know the strength of your brand, you have an assessment of the job cut out for you. Weakling and Aspiring brands are asking for a lot of work to become respectable. Formidable and Cult brands will come with huge responsibility and unless you are up to the task, you can seriously endanger their brand equity.

The other significant aspect you must be aware of is the stage at which your brand rests in its development cycle or its brand life cycle. Appreciation of this reality will allow you to strategize more effectively. The situation of your brand can vary at different stages as per the figure below.

On the X axis we plot time in years, on the Y is the growth of the brand (revenue) over the last few years. You can get various situations as depicted in the S-shaped graph below.

Figure 2.2: Brand life cycle

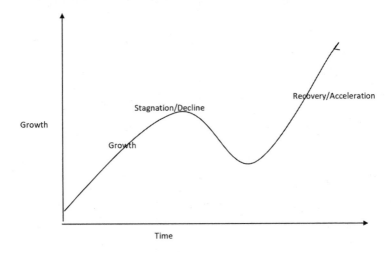

If your brand is clocking steady growth but is way short of reaching its potential, it's most likely in growth phase. Of course, if it's declining, the line would be pointing southwards. If growth is petering out and you get a more flattish line, then your brand is stagnating and from there it can either decline or go up. Decline could lead to eventual extinction; conversely, recovery can lead to acceleration of growth and the brand may exhibit growth levels comparable to its initial years. The implications of each phase are very different for the brand manager.

- In the growth phase, you need to intensify consumer interactions so your brand builds scale by doing more of essentially the same thing that is obviously working well for you. Consumer need is well understood and articulated, and consumers are turning up at your door to enlist for your offering.
- If revenue is going south, then brands have to step back and re-evaluate their product or service. Diagnostics will reveal if consumers know, appreciate and value your offering as superior and distinctive from the ones currently available from competitors. Unless corrections are made, the brand will not inflect upwards. Long-standing brands (such as the apparel brand American Eagle even carry the proud rubric 'since year 1977' to signify their timeless success) have the inherent ability to stay relevant to their consumers in evolving times.
- If correction is made, brands can start to sputter upwards again. An indication of healthy growth is when their growth is ahead of category growth, implying that they are leading the need-satisfaction ahead of competitors. If not, stagnation will result in extinction.

The harsh truth of the world of brands is that there is no staying steady. You either go up or down. Your work is onerous in both cases because the demands are stiff either way.

So now that you know the strength of the brand, qualitatively speaking and the stage of its life cycle, quantitatively testified, it's time to start organizing your brand information so you can make the right choices.

Brand fact-o-file

Learning everything about the brand is seminal to dominating the agenda of your brand. In other words, let's make a brand fact-o-file comprising:

- *Imperatives:* Refreshing the concepts learnt on MBA campus, if you have been to one, so we know which ones to focus on amongst the host of ideas learnt. This also comprises a host of factual information that you must always be on top of.
- *Differentiators:* Adding other considerations that we have benefitted from working in the real world, which will give you an early edge and will also help you lead with a vision of the future.

Both of these will not only put you in control of your brand but also instil a punch in your thinking that others will find difficult to match, as you easily conquer one peak after another.

In the next two weeks, let's start from the outside and move in bit by bit, but lay a strong foundation brick by brick.

First understand the environment you are operating in. The concepts of economics that are of great use, but are shoddily factored into management thinking till much later, need to structure early in our thinking. Brand managers deal with consumer demand, the most indeterminate of all things, with the least interest in the outside world, although that's what influences the consumer's buying power.

Therefore, we recommend doing the following quick check on economy.

- *Growth rates*: Consider the country's GDP rate in the past and the projection for the current year. Linking this up with the category one works in early on will help us understand the macro-micro linkages that impact the demand of your brand in an intricate, inter-connected way. Try to correlate this with the category growth and brand growth and get used to asking yourself: 'Is my brand rising with the economy, going ahead of it or is it lagging behind?' Then ask yourself the same question for the category and the following implications will emerge if you subtract brand growth from category growth:
  o Brand growth more than category growth and GDP growth: favourable situation that is endorsing current strategy
  o Brand growth less than category growth: Need to get more competitive, whether or not brand growth is more or less than GDP growth
  o Brand growth less than GDP growth: a matter of serious concern since GDP growth is a macro indicator and category is its minuscule sub-set. Hence, a serious attempt should be made to either grow share (if you are not the leader) or the category (if you are the leader).

- *Inflation*: Understanding inflation will help you appreciate the pricing compulsions of your brand and their commensurate impact on volumes. Since pricing is mostly built on a cost plus model (wherein input costs are topped up with a margin expectation to arrive at desired MRP), pricing of raw material is bound to impact price and value perception of the brand, and brand custodians need to know and anticipate this situation.

  Also, since growth in value terms is the sum total of volume growth and pricing, it's important that brand managers have a real perception of what is real growth (measured in terms of volume growth or consumer transactions over the previous year on a comparable time scale) and what is inflated growth because of the sheer price increase with the same consumer transactions as last year. Increase in consumer transactions is the number of consumer purchases of a company's selling units over two comparable years with all things staying the same. An increase in consumer transactions indicates an authentic increase of brand adoption and purchase.

- *Industry situation*: Starting from the most distant to the most proximal industry to one's category, an appreciation of what's happening to your industry and around is an absolute must. For instance, if your category is chocolate, you need to start from industrial growth, then move to FMCG or fast-moving consumer goods industry, and following that, zero down to food industry, then snacks industry and finally focus on the chocolates and confectionery category. There is usually a strong correlation amongst these, and early signs of slowdown or growth can be detected if one is watching from the outside to the inside. If sometimes your category is inversely correlated, meaning others are declining but your category is growing, it will be important to know the reasons and protect and grow them rather than enjoy the good fortune and be taken by surprise later.

- *Company situation*: Your brand is a room in the house of your company. It's absolutely important to know how the house is faring to understand the health of one's room. Several brands comprise the portfolio of a company and often brand choices are made to suit the portfolio needs, not individual requirements of a brand. For instance, to report favourable results at an aggregated level, companies may compromise growth or profitability on individual brands although the need of the brand is high. This is often not desirable but somewhat inevitable because of the collective reality of the business you work in.

If the company is listed, one can get a sense of how it is doing by looking at basic indicators like:

o Stock price movements: for the last one year or last few quarters, along with analyst reports to get an outside sense of how the company's competitiveness is perceived.

o P/E ratio: or price or market value of the stock (obtained from the stock market listings, which is calculated by dividing the earnings per share—net profit in a fiscal year divided by number of shares). A high P/E ratio could mean that the company's stock is over-valued or investors are expecting high growth rates in future. A low P/E ratio shows that the company's value creation model is slowing down. Simply speaking, the ratio tells you how many years it would take to recover the cost of the share basis the earnings accruing to an investor every year, and is a good indicator of the financial health of the company.

- *Portfolio reality*: Continuing from above, one has to understand one's brand's standing in the light of other brands in the portfolio. For this we put growth of a company's brands on the X axis, and profit on the Y axis. This is unlike the BCG matrix which plots market share versus market growth to estimate the future potential of the portfolio, whereas here our interest is to understand the contribution of the respective brand in the portfolio of a firm.

Figure 2.3: Brand within company portfolio

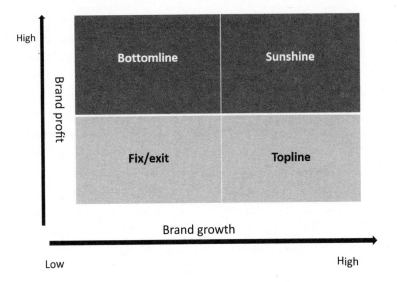

If your brand is in the top quadrant, you will enjoy 'sunshine' as you generate more revenue and profit, allowing investments to flow through. If not, you will either be squeezed for 'bottom line' or profit improvement, or 'top line' or revenue growth. If you are neither, you need to 'fix' or 'exit' your brand. The figure above indicates the choices that your brand is likely to face.

Now that we have some sense of the outside world, it's time to dissect the brands to complete the brand fact-o-file. Since brand management is a nodal function, all roads of purchasing, manufacturing, selling and finance lead up to marketing. People look to you for guidance; hence, having a bird's-eye view of business is critical at an early stage, even if you don't know all the details and even if you can't impact all the aspects of business. Here is what you must pack in your rucksack, before you start your climb for more growth and more profit.

Sales analysis: Look at your internal figures and understand your total brand turnover stated in net sales (usually net of taxes and margins to retail and distribution points), which measures the actual cash flowing into the company's coffers. It's important to also know what percentage of your company's sales comes from your brand. You could be a dominant player in your company bringing heavy sales with maximum share, or a small player with little volume but high growth, making you strategically important (especially if you are playing in the field where the company wants to grow and has core competitiveness in that sector), or you could be neither, becoming an insignificant me-too. It's important to know how much weight you and your brand carry in the organization as a result of your brand's situation. It will help you understand your strengths and weaknesses as a business and use this well to strike cross-alliances in your company to impact your brand's fortunes favourably.

For instance, if you bring in a lot of revenue, you are far likely to be a favourite of the sales director than the CFO and conversely, if you bring in profit, you are likely to be the CFO's favourite rather than the sales director's. You could use your inherent strength or weakness to reinforce or improve your situation. We will see more of this later.

After this, follow-up with variant sales since you could have many line extensions (like different flavours of Maggi noodles) or brand extensions (same brand but in a different category like Horlicks biscuits, as an extension of the core Horlicks Health Food Drink [HFD]). Know the percentage contribution and the profit contribution of each to the total brand sales. Combined with overall growth over the last two to three years, and growth in market share of the variants, you can make a good estimate of what to push and what not to, depending on the situation at hand.

Below is what your first brand fact-o-file grid could look like. Make an Excel sheet for yourself during the day, between your various jobs, and start filling this up assiduously. This is your fundamental brand knowledge for building brand power.

In the hypothetical example below of Lay's with only illustrative data (not real), we start with understanding the size of the brand, its variants, along with the growth they are registering, also seen in the light of the profitability. Also, we evaluate the size of our brand in the company's portfolio, to estimate the relative standing.

Figure 2.4: Portfolio growth/margin

Growth/ margin	Lay's				
Brand contribution	Chips	Baked chips	Stax	Crisps	Total
Total sale— INR crore	2000	20	75	50	2145
Per cent share in the company	40	10	6	8	64
Growth over last year— GOLY (per cent)	15	45	8	200	27
Gross margin (per cent)	45	50	55	57	52

All figures in the above chart are for illustration purposes only.

This allows one to know which variants to push and which to just de-prioritize with respect to both growth and profitability. For instance, Lay's Chips are growing slow compared to others but because of its sheer size, it contributes significantly to overall turnover. Whereas Crisps are small but seem to show a lot of potential. Baked chips are clearly stagnating, requiring a good look and Stax are small but because of Pringles' presence in this category, Frito-Lay may make a strategic call to keep its toehold in this category. From a profitability perspective, all are favourable but if the portfolio leans towards Crisps, then it will see a significant improvement.

The above grid, with a little bit of analysis, allows brand managers to understand the importance of macro analysis to make better trade-offs within the variants available on their brand. Managers who embed farsightedness in their strategic thinking invariably grow both top line and bottom line in the long term by making judicious choices at different times.

Above, we spoke about GOLY or growth over last year. We need to understand three other metrics for sales evaluation. While they are carelessly bandied about in boardrooms, the rigour in understanding them and their correlation is weak. Here is a quick glance at MTD, YTD, MAT, GOLY:

- MTD or month till date stands for the sales in a month over the same month last year. Or it is December 2020 sales growth over December 2019 by dividing the latter by the former. This is useful for calculating sales increases in one Republic Day or a Christmas over another year because the dates are fixed. But for Indian festivals which shift from year to year, MTD does not suffice. However, if you have put a specific sales drive in a month, then this metric helps one evaluate the specific uplift in that month over the same month last year, which ends up becoming a base year for calculation.

- YTD or year to date, which means cumulative sales in the year till the current month, becomes a better measure than MTD. Though in the first month of the year YTD is equal to MTD, subsequently, as time passes by, YTD reflects the year's performance more and more comprehensively as it covers more months or data points to give an aggregated picture where unusual increases and decreases are ironed out to yield a more uniform picture.

- GOLY or growth over last year is equal to YTD till a point of time. But if you want to consider previous years or estimate projected sales of this year over last year, GOLY becomes useful. It's a great indicator of a brand's performance over a long time period. As the time horizon expands, occasional bumps due to erratic demand situations are ironed out, yielding a more satisfactory understanding of the long-term trend.

- MAT or moving annual total (sometimes called monthly average total) is the cumulative sales of the last twelve months over the similar twelve months last year. Thus if you are in October 2019, you would look at sales of twelve months or October 2018 to September 2019 to get twelve months, and divide this by the same months or October 2017 to September 2018. MAT is a more dynamic measure and regardless of when you are measuring your performance, whether you are in January or October, you get an average of twelve months. Since companies follow the January–December cycle, the annual view is unavailable at any mid-point. MAT allows brand and sales purveyors to take annual stock and make appropriate decisions over seeing a longer trade-off with consumers. Also when you plot moving MAT month-wise in a graph, you get very robust data of how the business is moving over a year, but measured month after month. Thus MAT ends up being both statistically robust (since it covers an average of twelve months which is a long period versus a few months) and dynamic (since it's measured every month). MAT therefore gives a more long-term view of business and is a good way to determine the sustainability of a brand's performance.

This brings us to the last metric: CAGR or cumulative annual growth rate. This tells you simply how well you are accelerating or decelerating over the previous few years. For instance, if your growth rate over the last four years is 4 per cent, 6 per cent, 4 per cent and 8 per cent, then your CAGR is 5 per cent as a compounded growth indicator. CAGR is an excellent indicator of a company's performance over a longer period and is a priceless tool for analysts who analyse across firms and industries. The only hitch is that it blurs the detail that your performance has been somewhat bumpy over the years.

CAGR is used for estimating how your brand is doing vis-à-vis the market. Market underperformance or market overperformance is a measure of that and it's arrived at by simply subtracting brand growth from category growth. If the result is positive, celebrate, because your brand is ahead in its category. If it's negative, then you are trailing behind competition and it's time for introspection. However, if you are the market leader with a share upwards of 50 per cent, then you should worry about tepid growth because, being the largest contributor to the category, you have slowed it down.

A related example, akin to BDI and CDI (brand development index and category development index) which is taught in campuses but not applied well, is brand leadership or brand followership. We have simplified this because, as a brand manager, your role and outlook is very different in each case.

- In brand leadership, you lead the category. Hence, your job is to create new reasons for consumption with an ever-expanding base of patrons.
- In brand followership, where you are second or lower in the category, your job is to grab market share since it's easier and more economical to wean consumers away from competitors' brands, as they are already users of the category.

Only if you intend to disrupt the category from the outside by redefining the usage and relevance of the existing category through new codes of consumption, is your marketing objective likely to not fall into the above two types. For example, when mobile companies launched their services, they were not targeting their predecessors' pager users, but users of the broadest set of telecom services: landline users.

Now that we have discussed growth measurement, let's see how we organize data on relevant axes and then analyse it for identifying growth opportunities.

For this we have gone granular and converted sales volumes into percentages to be able to compare different variables and make meaningful inferences. The data has been sliced into:

- SKU (stock keeping unit)/region contribution and total pack-wise contribution showing us how the volume of SKUs is distributed across the country.
- SKU/region growth matrix indicating how SKUs are growing across the region.
- SKU/market share matrix which shows how the market share of Lay's is vis-à-vis Bingo, Balaji, etc.

Brand management requires that we look at the most relevant variables and simplify them so they can be seen in one glance to facilitate a decision, considering maximum variables that are relevant for the opportunity in question.

Now if you are seeking more growth, the question is where—which SKU will you choose to focus on and where is market share gain likely to accrue from that. Without getting paralysed by excessive analysis, we must choose the right geography that is showing signs of growth with the right SKU and gain share in the category where it's most likely to accrue. Below are the tables for your scrutiny before we arrive at some findings to maximize sales.

Figure 2.5: SKU/region contribution matrix

SKU/region contribution	North	South	West	East	Total	Pack Contribution
Small pack— Rs 10	20%	25%	18%	37%	100%	30%
Mid—Rs 20	30%	17%	18%	35%	100%	15%
Regular— Rs 30	40%	20%	25%	15%	100%	20%
Large— Rs 50	45%	25%	25%	5%	100%	35%
Total brand/ region contribution	30%	23%	20%	27%	100%	100%

All figures in the above chart are for illustration purposes only.

Looking at Figure 2.5, first we can read the following about our brand: from the extreme right column and the bottom row, it's clear that North and East are the biggest markets for Lay's and small packs and large packs are the biggest contributors to sales. Then, reading column-wise, we can see that North gets more sales from larger SKUs (mid and large), whereas East is the opposite, getting its sales from small and mid. West has more equitable distribution and South gets heavy sales from small and large packs at the extreme ends. These trends are early pointers to consumer understanding. Is East more value-conscious? Does North have heavy consumers and does South have something peculiar about small and large pack consumption, like a different habit or a rapidly expanding penetration? Analysis like this should get you thinking about reading the hidden patterns to ascertain your brand's differential appeal across regions.

But before you go on to make any decision to act on it, you must have an understanding of how the growth has been in the segments of the grid above. After all, you don't want to make a hasty inference basis volume–region distribution only. You plot your data and below is what you get for GOLY for the same variables.

Figure 2.6: SKU/region growth over last year matrix

SKU/region growth over last year	North	South	West	East	Total Pack-wise growth
Small pack—Rs 10	15%	12%	20%	25%	18%
Mid—Rs 20	18%	12%	8%	10%	12%
Regular—Rs 30	25%	8%	4%	8%	10%
Large—Rs 50	27%	30%	35%	6%	29%
Total region growth	22%	12%	15%	18%	17%

All figures in the above chart are for illustration purposes only.

Looking at Figure 2.6, reading this time from the bottom row up, and column-wise from the right, we can infer with a bird's-eye view that the large pack and North region are leading growth. Now as we go row-wise, we can see that there is maximum growth in the large pack, led by West and South. But at this point, we should realize that, apart from growth, we also have to be aware of which are the big markets for the large pack. This will lead us to read Figures 2.5 and 2.6 together and we realize that North is high too, considering it has the largest base for the category. Small pack is growing the most in East in spite of being a large market (37 per cent from Figure 2.5), followed by West, which is the smallest market. Mid pack and regular packs are growing less, with East and West pulling the growth down. This may be worth addressing as they are undermining growth.

As we complete our picture, the next logical question is how am I doing versus the category? For this we have to turn to market share and decide where we want to focus to regain lost share or where we have to consolidate and hold. Now we plot the market share in the same SKU/region table as below.

Figure 2.7: SKU/market share

SKU/market share	North	South	West	East	Total
Small pack—Rs 10	80%	60%	55%	70%	74%
Mid—Rs 20	55%	60%	62%	45%	58%
Regular—Rs 30	72%	70%	58%	69%	62%
Large—Rs 50	75%	55%	72%	60%	63%
Total	70%	62%	65%	62%	66%

All figures in the above chart are for illustration purposes only.

While Lay's is the market leader with a towering 66 per cent share, North and East are leaders with around 65 per cent share and West and South see more competition from local players as well as ITC.

So, with this understanding, if you are seeking more growth for your brand, where would you put your money (we will come to how later) so your impact is maximized? Now is the time to put these three tables together and draw meaningful inferences so data starts to read like a well-pieced-together story. Often managers don't analyse sufficient variables to acquire the confidence to have a point of view or they cut data in so many ways that they either get fatigued or lose sight of inferring sufficiently. It's important that you read the data as widely as possible and infer as cohesively as possible to avoid the extremes of analysis–paralysis, and its lesser-known cousin, analysis–negligence.

You can skin this data in many ways, but we are indicating the top three for you to consider. Then put your own and prioritize (you know the actual volumes behind these when you calculated the percentages) the top three to execute.

- The market is biggest in North and East, where our market share is high. We should continue the bull run here by maximizing whatever is working—TV media, distribution, digital engagement . . . Remember, if you drop your guard here, the volume drop will impact total brand growth.
- Lead in East with small pack where the growth rate is high and where you also enjoy substantial size, and with large pack in North. This will not only allow you to further grow your market share on an already expanded base, but will also help you lead the category invincibly.
- For West, which contributes 23 per cent, continue your great work with large pack (you are growing at 35 per cent with a 72 per cent share), but crack your mid and regular pack where growth is struggling in single digits and market share is hovering around the 60s. Find a way through innovation or distribution to crack the market. For South, which is your third biggest market, you have to work beyond your large pack which is growing well, and evaluate a focused drive on small and mid-sized packs, since your market share is also low, indicating the problem is with your brand, not the category.

If you are feeling, 'Phew, I have had enough', then look at this data with respect to different flavours' contribution as below, and start taking notes again on clear growth pointers.

Tired? Well, marketing is an iterative science hung between quantitative grind and qualitative estimations. The more you can learn to crunch numbers and abstract for trends, the better you will become at analysing and coming up with solutions. Otherwise, you are either a number-cruncher or a gut-feel-prescriber, lacking both rigour and imagination to make a difference to your brand.

Figure 2.8: Flavour/region cross tab

Flavour/ region contribution	North	South	West	East	Total	Contribution/ total
Classic Salted	20%	27%	10%	43%	100%	35%
Magic Masala	40%	22%	20%	18%	100%	25%
Cream Onion	20%	25%	33%	22%	100%	27%
Tomato Tango	20%	26%	37%	17%	100%	13%
Total	100%	100%	100%	100%	100%	100%
Contribution/ total	30%	23%	20%	27%	100%	

All figures in the above chart are for illustration purposes only.

To get you started, before we take a qualitative jump in the next chapter for your next week, here are a few pointers:

- Classic Salted is the biggest flavour, followed by Cream Onion.
- North loves Magic Masala, West loves Tomato Tango (sweet palate of consumers, perhaps), East prefers Classic Salted and South has a uniform taste preference.
- So if North and East are the biggest contributors to the business (as from previous tables also) and South and West need to be nurtured, what is your flavour strategy going to be?
- And, how would you grab share from competitors—maybe it's time to pull out one more table of market share and supplement the above data.
- And, if your CFO asked you to prioritize the bottom line for the next quarter, do you have leeway to push one flavour over the other? But have you checked the gross margin before to know

which flavour yields better returns for your business for the same unit sales of flavours?

Another thing you need to be aware of while doing regional evaluation of your business is the Nielsen retail report. Usually, if you are able to set up a good numeric distribution target, or distribution spelt out in the number of outlets that you want covered, and follow up on it tenaciously, you get an improvement in your brand availability. But sometimes, you need to question if you are going to the right outlets, or to those that contribute a higher amount of the sales of your category. You will need to refer to Weighted Distribution. This refers to percentage measurement of your sales upon category sales in the outlets that index high on sales of your category. Three situations can emerge if you are analysing numeric and weighted distribution together as you expand distribution.

- Numeric is up and also weighted: This means your brand is not only going to more outlets but is also going to the right outlets.
- Numeric is up but weighted is either stagnant or dropping: This means the effort of your sales team is not adding up as they are adding marginal outlets where the category sells less. This means increased operational complexity but not enough sales.
- Numeric is low but weighted is growing: This could be acceptable if you are attempting to consolidate your brand sales because you are getting more returns for less coverage which can improve your return on investment on distribution. If that is not the case, then please invest in growing numeric distribution.

If, from the above analysis, you were wondering what gross margin really means, then let's take this up in the next chapter, but not before switching to the right side of the brain so we can balance our learning.

Week 3 and 4

What Does the Consumer Need?

Managerial skill: Improviser

After understanding the researcher mentioned in the STRIVES framework in the previous chapter, it's time to understand and develop the functional skill of the Improviser. The one who takes every project, every task and lifts it from being mediocre to being spectacular, with outstanding attention to detail. How does one develop this skill to make the most of the situation and have a relentless appetite for improvement? Develop the traits below or, if you don't have them, look for people who can supplement you with these valuable features.

- *Detail tasks within tasks:* Improvisers are known for looking at the whole picture of many intricate interconnecting pieces in ways that creators don't (we will cover this later). A product for them is instantly full of opportunities to optimize ingredient costs, manufacturing intricacies, logistics challenges, new technologies . . . they excel in seeing between the lines and even beyond it. If you want to be an improviser, then develop the eye for unbundling the product and service inherent in your brand into meaningful parts and isolate them from each other so you can break your task to improve into bite-sized pieces.

-   *Prioritize:* Their ability to look at detail is not squandered by a reckless pursuit of the minutiae. Improvisers know what matters and what doesn't. Likewise, understand what elements of the project you have decomposed deliver to the final objective you are chasing. For instance, if you are redesigning a product recipe, then ask yourself which aspects of raw material or packaging costs have maximum impact on reducing costs without undermining quality on desirable parameters. Only then tinker with those elements where effort is commensurate with returns or else you could distract resources without amounting to much. If prioritization is not judicious, it can dispirit your team, leading eventually to abandonment of the task.

-   *Rally resources, allocate roles, monitor:* Assuming you have understood the various sub-tasks inherent in a task, whether it's product design, cost improvement or bettering service delivery, it's time to look for resources and deploy them behind the projects with an equitable distribution of responsibilities in keeping with people's capabilities and interests, and review them from time to time to monitor progress.

-   *Set clear objectives and timelines:* Since improvisations have many niggling details, it's important that the final objectives and the smaller objectives that feed into the big one are clear with established timelines. This way, the different parts of the project will add up and not disintegrate the larger picture.

Improvisation is an absolutely critical skill to make the most of existing resources for delivering to an objective. Brand managers who excel in this skill are able to maximize returns for their business and are extremely valuable in most business situations with their ability to prioritize.

Consumer need: the holy grail of marketing

A disproportionate emphasis on consumer need is perhaps all right in the domain of marketing. The deeper the consumer need is understood, the more often it is brought to bear on brand discussions. Business discussions can often get very elliptical and inconclusive, but if consideration of consumer need is kept foremost, solutions can follow fairly easily.

In general parlance, need, want, desire and demand are used interchangeably, but for marketers these words need to be dissected to unravel the nuances within. Need is a craving that humans feel inside, impelling them into action, but it tends to be somewhat diffused. It operates at a subliminal level and craves fulfilment. If catered to, it leads to satisfaction. If neglected or missed, it creates discontent, or expresses itself in some other way. But its tug is so palpable, that it necessitates yielding to.

Need is somewhat ambiguous till it passes through the lens of a specific yearning to become a want. So, you need to slake your thirst, but you are uncertain or not particular about how to satisfy it. At this point, you start to have some vague idea of what you want with some detail but you are open to having a conversation. Or you may want something but there is a hurdle towards getting it. This is where marketers step in. If you have a broad craving for a category, they convert that into the demand for their brand. Or if the category is not in the consumer's consideration, they bring it up so it becomes foremost.

Conversion of want to demand therefore requires holding the consumer's hand in two ways:

- Finding the **barrier** that the consumer is facing, articulating it for them, and eliminating it so they are able to access the brand experience. For instance, you could remind the consumer that he is unable to sleep well because existing mosquito repellents don't last all night and you have a solution that works twenty-four hours.

- Promise a functional and emotional **benefit** such that their diffused wants become an opportunity for a satisfying experience. Here the consumer is attracted with a benefit bigger than they expected, causing them to demand your product. For example, when a consumer is thirsty on a hot day, indicate to them to not merely drink water but enjoy the mysterious satisfaction of Pepsi that uplifts them and enables them to get more in life, wherever they may be or whatever they might be doing. The promise of the benefit can be and is usually exaggerated because it's meant to create high expectations so consumers demand more. But done consistently, it becomes a reality for the consumer, affecting their lives as the brand desires.

Brands that consistently work on debottlenecking the barrier and delivering a promise stay both relevant and desirable. The road of relevance and desirability eventually lands the brand into an iconic status so it's good for marketers to be industrious towards this cause.

Below is the explanation of this Need-Want-Barrier/Benefit-Demand (NWB/BD) pathway that every marketer must continuously walk and get better at, every day of his working life. It would be worthwhile to pause and digest this difference before we go one step deeper into need and want to impact the demand for our brand.

Figure 3.1: Need-want-barrier/benefit-demand pathway

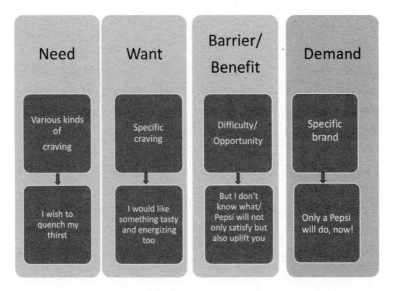

Adept marketers go deep into the desire, decode the need, convert that into a want for their brand and raise the demand for it by promising benefits that make their offer irresistible. Deep-rooted brand loyalty invariably stems from a fundamental understanding of human desire, whereas superficial brand loyalty is merely based on a passing demand of the moment. To that extent, understanding the intricacies of the NWB/BD pathway helps anchor the brand as far back into a fundamental need, and as far ahead into the consumer satisfaction that creates an insistent demand for it.

Need has so far been understood on the basis of Maslow's hierarchy of ranking human urges. This is what it looks like for a quick revision:

Figure 3.2: Maslow's need-hierarchy model

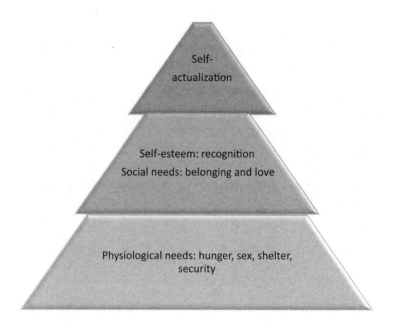

But this model only captures the positive wants. Whereas we know that, apart from positive motivations, we are also driven by negative emotions: doubt, anxiety, fear, dread. For converting a need to a want, it's important to look at both. Saffola drove the conversion for their heart-friendly oil through fear of an imminent cardiac disaster, or Tide does it these days through the fear of losing out on a job opportunity because of poor presentation of oneself. Avoiding an oncoming disaster is as potent a tool to draw consumers to a brand, as is attracting them with a gilded opportunity. So we have expanded Maslow's need to the haunts, apart from the wants, that it generates.

Thus, marketers can reflect both positive wants and negative haunts of consumers, as explained below in the context of Pepsi:

- Physiological: you can satisfy your thirst or be left parched
- Social and self-esteem: be loved by all, making you feel good or left in oblivion
- Self-actualization: feel uplifted, moving towards creativity, or be perpetually in need and stay unable to realize one's potential

Below is the grid, which when applied to various categories, can yield a rich set of consumer wants and haunts that can be leveraged.

Figure 3.3: Want-Haunt model

Maslow's need	Want ('I wish')	Haunt ('I dread')
Physiological	food, security, sex	hunger, homelessness, loneliness
Social	loved	destitute
Self-esteem	respected	despised, insignificant
Self-actualization	worthiness	meaninglessness

The conversion from want to an unrelenting demand when consumers are willing to queue up outside a retail outlet waiting for the shop to open happens, but it requires understanding barriers and promising benefits that consumers will be showered with if they embrace the brand. Let's first understand the benefits.

Benefits can be material, based on the features of the product or service, like the faster computing of the Intel chip or the weight-managing, well-being proposition of Kellogg's Special K. But functional benefits really acquire an insurmountable tug when they cue emotional benefits. Therefore, brand marketers must allude overtly or covertly towards that emotional satisfaction which will be met upon consumption of the brand.

So, what are the various emotions that humans experience? There are many, but we have zeroed down on the six basic emotions for you to bear in mind when you are asking yourself what consumer emotions are you pandering to. As you would notice in Figure 3.4 below, there are four positive and two negative emotions. But now, following the want or haunt model, or craving or fear of consumers, we have corresponding positive and negative emotions also.

Marketers work usually on the positive side as they want the brands to be harbingers of positive change, but negative emotions also work well sometimes. It helps them realize the consequence of ignoring a pressing need, like healthcare, and nudges them into taking action in favour of the brand.

Figure 3.4: Wheel of emotions

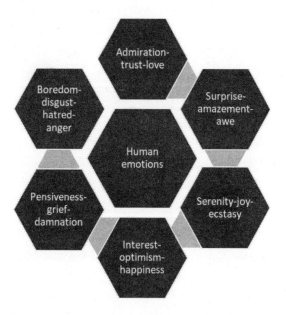

Brands must be able to promise emotional benefits: ensure positive emotions and avoid negative ones to convert the want into demand. The prospect of positive emotional pay-off makes a brand's lure compelling. However, even if consumers want the benefits, it may yet not convert into demand because there are 'barriers' which come in the way.

Barriers may be physical, such as a lack of electricity, creating a market for inverters; or they may be personal where consumers are unable to overcome a personal diffidence to realizing their goals, paving the way for Fair (oops, Glow) and Lovely; or they may be social when society prevents women from embracing new roles or continuing their old ones due to motherhood, giving rise to the business opportunity of crèches for infants.

Mining the barriers towards need-fulfilment is an important step in converting the want into a compelling demand. This takes us to the next elusive aspect of tapping consumer demand: consumer insight.

Consumer insight: the heart of marketing

Consumer insight mining enables a brand manager to get a perspective on the following:

- The real consumer need that is at work. If it's unarticulated or is dormant, it can be expressed
- Understand what consumers want and what haunts them
- Find the barriers coming in the way of want-fulfilment or haunt-annulment
- And estimate the emotional pay-off that would convert the want into a compelling demand

However, this seems simpler to state than to deduce. The whole set of consumers seem to talk in different voices, have fragmented ideas and sometimes, lack the time or motivation, or worse still, may not even articulate what they really want or dread.

A host of techniques are deployed, therefore, to understand how to satisfy the consumer. Through in-depth one-to-one probing, from focus groups to projective techniques, consumers' real motivations and barriers are elicited. From these, the consumer insight is drawn. The process involves gathering a set of consumer **statements**, then sifting them into a broad set of **inferences** and stringing them together to understand their needs, wants, haunts, benefits and barriers to convert their want into demand for the brand. Below is an example of consumer insight, which was the basis for the launch of Quaker Oats + Milk, Almond Flavour ready-to-drink beverage.

The consumer statements that were picked after collating consumer research were: 'I like oats but the drink is very sticky'; 'Oatmeal for breakfast is not easy to make when I am rushing to office, and it's also very time-consuming to eat'; 'I find oats with milk somewhat heavy for the morning; however, after I have left home for office, I feel I can eat it'; 'I find the taste of oats too bland for my liking.'

Some more statements went as follows: 'I know it's not the healthiest choice but I have an energy drink early in the day to keep me going'; 'I like oats and milk but find the idea of spooning it up at a breakfast table very boring'; 'No time for a healthy meal in the day, I have to rush off'; 'Oats and milk is a great nutritious idea for a sportsperson, but I need to have it every day and it's too cumbersome to make it'; 'In its current format, it's really for older people, in need of serious nutrition, not me, who needs an everyday solution.'

Now these random statements can be bucketed as follows, making terse consumer inferences for the next stage. These are:

- Oats + Milk is great but it's cumbersome to make, time-consuming to eat.
- Oats + Milk is heavy, so it should be consumed a bit after breakfast, perhaps when on the way to office.
- Oats + Milk has a boring taste and an inconvenient backward format for consumption.

- Other options, though less healthy, are convenient and end up becoming my preferred choice.
- Oats + Milk is not for youngsters, not modern, not for everyday consumption.

From the above, we identify the physiological need for healthy nutrition; the want for tasty, on-the-go, more contemporary presentation. We discover the barrier of being seen as old-fashioned and unsuitable for modern times and me.

If we now bridge the inferences with the barriers, we come to an expression of **consumer insight** that states not only what they yearn for but also why they are not getting it. For this, we have to capture the spirit of all of the above, which would wrap up as:

'I wish I had a healthy, tasty and convenient format that was easy to consume in the mornings, befitting my everyday need without seeming very old-world.'

The above statement expresses all of the above, in essence, and also the barriers that need to be unlocked to enable the consumer to embrace your brand. Now if we top this up with emotional benefits from our want-haunt model of positive or negative emotions, we can convert this want into a demand with a compelling reason. In this case, Sachin Tendulkar was brought in to infuse modernity and cue benefits of exceptional fitness in everyday life.

The process of consumer insight seems deceptively easy, but it can trip up the savviest marketers. Unless all of the wants are captured and captured entirely in spirit, the failure downstream can be inevitable. Hence, rigour must be applied along the entire consumer 'insighting' process to make prudent decisions after considering everything comprehensively.

So, back to our last brand fact-o-file before we move into the next week.

We did the sales analysis, now we have to quickly get on top of product details and financials, keeping the competition in mind, to close our first mile of the brand journey.

Brand P&L

Knowing how your product costs are structured is absolutely essential to running a brand, much like knowing the power of your car versus your arch rival's in Formula 1 racing. Not only does it equip you with the knowledge of your competitive strength or weakness, but it also tells you where you can shave costs that consumers don't value and channelize it into more engagement or promotion or innovation—which consumers always value more.

Below is a comparative table of your brand's (Lay's) and the competitor's (Bingo, for example) profit and loss statement. What observations do you draw that you can use to increase the impact of your brand for the consumer?

Figure 3.5: Comparative P&L

Figures in INR/unit	Your brand	Competitor brand
MRP	10	10
Net sales (less GST, margins, trade spend)	7.5	7.2
Raw material cost/unit	2.1	1.9
Packaging material cost/unit	0.7	0.6
Variable manufacturing cost/unit	1.2	1.4
COGS (cost of goods sold)	4	3.9

Figures in INR/unit	Your brand	Competitor brand
COGS (per cent of net sales)	53%	54%
Gross margin–Rs	3.5	3.3
Gross margin–(per cent of net sales)	47%	46%
Fixed marketing expense	0.35	0.6
Fixed distribution	0.8	0.8
Fixed factory	0.9	0.9
Marketing and general expenses	0.8	0.8
Net profit	0.65	0.2
Net profit (per cent of net sales)	9%	3%

All figures in the above chart are for illustration purposes only.

Running through the lines, we notice the relative strengths and weaknesses of our brand that point towards areas of improvement. Now, it may not always be possible to get your competitor's P&L but a dummy simulation can be done tapping the market intelligence of common vendors. It may seem tedious, even farcical at first, but it yields priceless inferences for keeping your brand ahead on the winning track.

- We can see in this case that Bingo buys the potatoes cheaper, which could be a result of ITC's better rates through backward integration or different specifications that are more accepting of lower grade potatoes (as processing can make up for poor potatoes' quality which consumers may not perceive).
- Lay's enjoys a lower manufacturing cost, perhaps a function of its economies of scale given its large manufacturing footprint,

but has a higher packaging cost. This poses the question, is the laminate over-specified and if yes, does it truly add to consumers' value perception? If not, this should be brought down (assuming no impact on shelf life of the product) and the savings used for more chips in the bag which gives better value to the consumer.

- Looking at the gross margin, we can see that the category enjoys good margins in the vicinity of 50 per cent, which is much higher than proximal categories like biscuits or confectionery. A healthy margin should be protected at all times, by reducing cost through pushing out inefficiencies and increasing price (or dropping grammage, given that consumers prefer even price points of INR 10 or 20) but simultaneously making the product worth the experience—better flavours, chipping experience, etc. Gaining an early appreciation of gross margins puts positive pressure to sustain the quality and superior experience of the product in an inflationary economy, so that consumers find it worth the price.

- Looking at other cost lines, one can see that the competitor is spending more on marketing as a percentage of sales. Though this may not be sustainable in the long run, given the low net profit of Bingo, but the Lay's brand manager needs to be ready with low share of voice, which can lead to market share erosion, and take counter measures, pre-emptively.

There are many other observations one can make looking at the P&L, some strategic, some tactical. A robust understanding of financials goes a long way in leading change, rather than being led by it.

A detailed analysis of one's cost at the manufacturing level is an absolute must to secure long-term competitive advantage and also secure sufficient marketing spends for one's brand. So, this time we do a deeper drill on the costs vis-à-vis a local player, Balaji. Increasingly, the competition is coming from local players who are challenging mainstream players with sharp cuts on cost.

Looking below, we can see that the cost of raw material is high for Lay's versus Balaji. Not all the costs of Balaji can be matched, but where it can be, a brand manager must challenge his stakeholders to help him lower costs. However, one has to be cautious in cutting costs to avoid losing what consumers value. Therefore it's important to retain what matters and communicate to consumers so they know why they are paying more, and drop what doesn't matter. For example, you may decide to retain the high cost flavour, but go for less stringent specifications on potato quality or look at your secondary packaging costs which clearly has no value for the consumer. Finally, a big brand like Lay's can have many non-working advertising and marketing (A&M) costs (these are defined as non-consumer-facing as against media which is consumer-facing and directly impacts consumption) that ought to be reduced with a military discipline, otherwise local, nimble players will most certainly make a market share gain at the expense of Lay's with lower A&M spends as shown below:

Figure 3.6: Cost-competitiveness comparison

Potato chips	Cost lines	Lay's	Balaji
		cost/kg (INR)	cost/kg (INR)
Net Sales/kg		750	650
Raw material (RM)	Potatoes	50	35
	Flavours	220	165
	Oil	30	25
	Others	30	20
	Total	330	235
Per cent		44%	36%

Potato chips	Cost lines	Lay's	Balaji
		cost/kg (INR)	cost/kg (INR)
Packaging material (PM)	Laminate	113	120
	Secondary packaging	52.5	45
A&M	Working A&M	55	8
	TV	40	0
	Digital, others	15	8
	Non-working A&M	7	5
	Production	4	2.5
	Research	3	2.5
	Total A&M	62	13
Per cent		8	2

All figures in the above chart are for illustration purposes only.

Where recipes are different, as in the case of Horlicks versus Pediasure, the brand manager should draw a comparative chart to understand the ingredient make-up and the relative strength of each product. This is important for building the positioning strength of one's brand on the basis of its composition vis-à-vis others, while making a constant effort to improve one's product in keeping with consumer trends. Often, managers can lose sight of the outside world, driven by internal compulsions and erode the appeal of their brand with consumers.

So, now that we have done a drill intersecting soft skills of unravelling a consumer's mind and looking at hard numbers in the business, it's time to go to the market so we can diagnose problems and devise solutions where the real battle between brands plays out.

Week 5 and 6

How Do I Diagnose a Problem?

Office art: Boss management

As we get into the fifth week, it's important to get into building some softer aspects of office art that defines the canvas quietly and shapes your career. We are starting with the one that is probably the most discussed but least managed, namely, boss management. Many a career has torpedoed into oblivion or catapulted to dizzying heights by the way people have managed their line manager. Performance does matter; never underestimate the importance of that. What matters equally, but is not realized, is what constitutes good performance. In other words, what is believed to be good performance, what is the right benchmark, what is the appreciation of the difficulties encircling the performance and the results that you have managed in spite of them.

So essentially, you need to be able to establish your framework for the fair appraisal of your success that is reflective of your ability and appreciative of your achievement potential. You don't want to fit into a random, unchallenged and almost accidental framework of evaluation within which your boss judges you; one that even she may not be aware of, but unconsciously acts out of. It's very important, therefore, to have a chance to set your framework of evaluation as much as going about your performance and waiting for a fair assessment.

Boss management includes displaying a few qualities that some possess fortuitously or others lack. To remove the element of chance, we recommend the following, because if you don't manage your boss well, there is little chance that you will manage the brand well. Brand management requires that you have a certain amount of independence and that senior management has faith in you; hence, it's important to pay heed to this critical aspect of your career.

First, the fundamentals of a boss. You don't choose your boss, she is given to you. This is known but its corollaries are not sufficiently understood. Don't expect your boss to change; it's not her problem if you don't vibe with her. Change yourself and adapt your style to hers to increase your chances of success. Don't surprise your boss with bad news, don't stay away from her for too long, and don't approach her only for your problems. Your boss needs to see you as a confidant, a problem-solver and one who pushes the agenda. She has to hear new ideas, better ways to solve the problems you are facing, and your initiatives to make it happen. So, please give her opportunities to see how you think, evolve consensus and get results, involving her actively or passively at all times. If you must take problems to your boss because of a bad situation, make sure you go with sufficient solutions and timelines to show light at the end of the dark tunnel.

If you follow these basics, you will have peace to work on your brand both in favourable and unfavourable situations.

Now the nuts and bolts of handling your boss. In your work, make sure you have conversations at appropriate points covering the following:

-   *Situation diagnosis*: we will work on brand diagnosis in the following chapter in detail, but make sure you sit with your boss and explain and win his concurrence on how good or bad the situation is. Being on the same page is important before you start a race with similar expectations, otherwise you can have a disaster on your hands. Make sure enough rigour has gone into the analysis so if he differs in the conclusion, he must have the knowledge that it's contrary to the data you are showing. That way it's clear at the start (though this alone may not be sufficient) what your recommendation was and how he or she chose otherwise. Though if this goes wrong, you may not be bailed out completely, but over time, bosses will realize their mistake and appreciate your view.

- *Expectations:* If there is some consensus on how the situation at hand is (it's better to do this sooner rather than later and if there is too much discordance, it's worth having another meeting to come to some consensus), then the imminent question is what the solution is, how much is to be done and how soon. Defining what the changed situation will look like is important to register realistic expectations whatever the state of business: turnaround, maintenance, expanding, start-up or mere re-aligning, as we have discussed earlier. Conversation should be around what is expected at the end of the evaluation period and one must at all times endeavour to underpromise and overdeliver rather than the other way round.

- *Resources:* You cannot climb Mount Everest in home gear. Business situations call for resourcing for success. If people, money, cross-functional support, top management sanction is weak, failure is only a matter of time. Make sure that the boss's early commitment to resource appropriately is taken. He or she may hesitate initially, but will come around to sanctioning it if the plan to succeed is well considered. Often managers hate to ask for resources fearing scaling up expectations that they may not be able to match. But this fear is unfounded because defining a situation and not asking for help to work on it is ill-fated from the start.

- *Modus operandi:* Once the hard numbers are defined, it's time to understand how the boss wants to interact on an ongoing basis. Does she prefer more informal frequent meetings or structured calendarized interactions? Many disasters have happened in spite of best intentions when wires criss-cross as your natural style is the opposite of your boss's.
- *Personal development:* Finally, all plans work well when you answer the imminent question, *What's in it for me?* Be clear to match the effort with rewards by clearly establishing what you stand to attain by doing your task well. Remember not only is the reward of elevation a great motivator for you but it also forces top management to review your performance and recognize you when the time comes. There is nothing worse than winning a race with no one around to commensurately reward you for the effort. Make sure also that you put sufficient ambition in your development and force the boss to evaluate you for higher roles so you truly gain, rather than settle for a measly promotion or salary increase that is not up to your liking.

Now that we are beginning to understand the boss-subordinate relation, it's time again to polish our brand competencies in week 5. Let's venture out.

Market challenge

Step into the market often. Step into the market as a discipline. Any seasoned marketer worth his salt would advise young marketers to do that early so it becomes ingrained. Office struggles can keep us indoors but the choice of battles to be waged and what it takes to win is determined only when we gain better appreciation of the place where the brand meets the consumer: retail.

Stepping out into the retail world, we can start to train our eyes to become live barometers of the brand, as we become live witnesses to brand sales in the competitive environment within the category and outside of it.

We looked at the shelves and classified the problems as follows:

1. Your brand presence—also called forward stock share (the number of packs visible on the shelf or the stock in the outlet of your brand versus the others)—is less than market share. For example, your market share is stated to be 30 per cent, but when you count the number of packs on the shelf of the category across a range of outlets, you find it lower than the total of the competitive packs. This means that you are under-represented now and are likely to lose market share in the future if the situation persists.

2. Your brand and other brands in the category are getting squeezed vis-à-vis some other category (this would require a few visits, or checking with the retailer, or obtaining scanned data from organized trade to corroborate occasionally). For instance, juices growing at the cost of carbonated beverages, or namkeens getting bigger than potato chips, or certain formats like cans growing in prominence over PET bottles.

3. You find that your brand has a presence but it's not quite as formidable as some other category that seems to enjoy disproportionate presence that even retailers favour as they report this enviable category is selling fast. You also want to grow as fast as that, unsatisfied by your current growth rate.

4. Your brand launched a new flavour or got into another category as a brand extension (like shaving cream after a shaving razor) but you find that your new product is not growing fast enough.

Our analysis reveals that the above problems, with some cross-validation from other syndicated research, can be typified as follows:

Figure 4.1: Fundamental brand issues

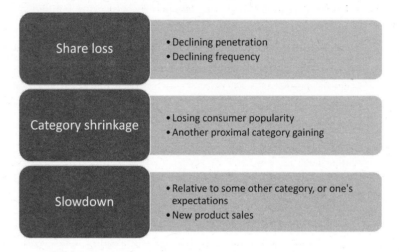

Losing market share (both volume and value, or either) could be as a market leader or as a follower. Either case is alarming since it reflects declining competitiveness which, if left unchecked, will lead to severe market share loss, even exclusion from a category.

Share loss

What are the indicators that your brand is losing share?

- Nielsen's sales reports and your internal reports will show a decline in GOLY, YTD, MAT and maybe MTD also. Nielsen can give a fairly detailed analysis of where and how market share is an issue, but if data is faulty, a quick retail panel with a select few outlets will validate the picture and give you a fairly good answer to the problem. Cross-validation with one's internal numbers will help extrapolate competitors' market share. For instance, if your sales data is under-represented by 40 per cent, then you can upweight your competitor's data by the same amount to get an accurate estimate of their sales.

- One has to then look at the HHP (household panel is a syndicated study that examines evolving consumer behaviour verified by actual purchase over a period of time) data to understand the movement of consumers within the category and outside. Gain and loss analysis which is provided by this research for Horlicks is shown below.

Figure 4.2: Gain and loss analysis (HHP)

Gain and loss—Horlicks	All India (Urban and Rural)	
Brand net shift volume	Feb '20	Feb '19
	-3550	-765
Entry to/lapse from category	645	1120
Addition/deletion from repertoire	-1400	400
Increase/decrease in consumption of brand	-1845	-1650
Total shift to/from brand	-950	-595
Pediasure	-150	-75
Bournvita	-450	-375
Complan	-200	-145

All figures in the above chart are for illustration purposes only.

The above table calibrates the movement of consumers from one period to another (in this case Feb '20 over Feb '19). As can be seen from this hypothetical example of Horlicks, it's losing volumes at an increasing rate (loss of 3550 unit volume versus 765 in the previous year), which is happening on account of the entry of new consumers into the category, stated in positive, being less than the previous year (645 versus 1120 last year). What makes it worse is that fewer consumers are holding on to Horlicks in their repertoire of consumption, which means a drop in penetration. And there is also a drop in depth of consumption (-1845 versus -1650, previous year: which also shows a continuing decline for two years) and loss of market share as Horlicks is losing in these consumer households (HHP verifies brand gain or loss by consumers' diary records validated by physical counting of packs) to Bournvita, Complan and Pediasure.

A drop in consumption is a tricky brand ailment. It simply means that existing consumers are having less of the product. Often U&A (Usage and Attitude) studies, conducted at a frequency of about three to four years, indicate the typical frequency of brand uptake and this is likely to show up there if corrective steps are not taken. A drop in frequency of consumption would take fresh research to understand the core reason for this. However, a few hypotheses can be suggested around which confirmatory research can be mounted and the exact reason can be established. Frequency of consumption could drop on account of:

-   Fatigue with the product based on taste or sheer monotony of consumption
-   Declining appeal of the concept of the product, which shows up in a lack of urgency in consumption over time, leading to a drop-out in severe cases
-   Gradual weaning away to competitors' products or even other categories. For example, consumers may occasionally flirt with another brand for a change of taste or even try other breakfast options like a cereal or a paratha or dosa or upma or poha (depending on which geography the consumer hails from) falling for the lure of the home culinary delights.

- Drop in belief of the efficacy of milk, the carrier of milk food drinks/health food drinks (MFD/HFD) due to the growing age of milk, fear of adulteration, etc.

The picture is quite alarming for a brand like Horlicks. So we can confirm further by looking at the trial rate (number of new entrants in one period over the total base of users), lapsage rate (how many people left the brand over the total base of users) and retention rate (how many people continued to consume over the total base of users) in percentage terms over one year, measured at the same time. Here the picture is consistent, showing a drop in trial, increase in lapsage and drop in retention rate.

Figure 4.3: Brand trial/lapsage/retention rate

Entry/Erosion	Feb '20	Feb '19
Trial rate	42%	48%
Lapsage rate	41%	40%
Retention rate	58%	62%

All figures in the above chart are for illustration purposes only.

We can also look at penetration data trends to evaluate how the brand is doing. Here we take a longer time period to see a pattern, since penetration data can be misleading if seen merely from one point to another. A more robust trend emerges from a trend line. If we take a longer set of data points and analyse this vis-à-vis base Horlicks and total Horlicks with its extensions included (Junior, Mother's, Woman's Horlicks), the pattern that emerges is as follows:

Figure 4.4: Category, brand penetration

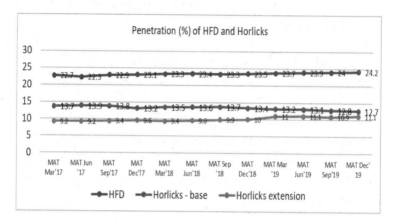

All figures in the above chart are for illustration purposes only.

It appears from the above figure taken over quarterly MATs that the HFD category is still growing but Horlicks base (the parent brand) is declining, whereas the extensions are doing all right.

Putting all this together, it clearly emerges that the brand's penetration needs to be bolstered and grown, otherwise the brand stands a real risk of losing out in popularity with consumers and share from competition.

After checking the drop in internal sales, market share and penetration, one can correlate with the brand health data and establish whether the brand needs to be fixed at a fundamental level. The brand health data typically captures the association of brands on a numeric scale along a few image parameters and looks as follows:

Figure 4.5: Brand track data

Brand image parameters	Q2 '18	Q3 '18	Q4 '18	Q1 '19	Q2 '19	Q3 '19	Q4 '19
Brand I trust	73	70	75	80	78	75	78
Brand the child asks for	75	73	70	78	72	74	72
Tastes best	78	80	82	83	80	83	82
Is scientifically formulated	75	74	73	72	73	74	78
Doctors recommend	77	65	72	70	63	68	70

All figures in the above chart are for illustration purposes only.

Brand attribute score changes have to be seen over time since the swings are slow and not always linear. From the above one can infer that Horlicks has gone up in 'taste' and 'scientific formulation', but isn't quite moving up on image attributes like 'Doctors recommend' or in kid appeal, while being somewhat flat in consumer trust.

All of these are alarming signals for the brand manager, urging her to seek diagnostics and get to work before the decline becomes severe and irreversible. We will see how this problem was fixed later in real life, but it's critical to identify the drop in brand scores at an early stage to address it expeditiously.

Category shrinkage

Category shrinkage signals start to appear when the leading brand in the category starts to show declining scores on brand equity parameters. Dropping scores on trust, value and product functionalities, such as the ones we saw in the case of share loss, will go to indicate that consumers are finding their category insufficient in meeting their demand.

For market leaders, it means that they have to protect the category, and if they don't lead the category narrative, they are likely to fall prey to marauding categories that prowl close to the category under attack.

What are the other signals for category shrinkage? From gain and loss analysis, as above, one can see that the total weight of the category, measured in units, is less in one period over the other. In that case the data would look as shown below, and research may have to be modified to capture which category is attracting consumers away from HFD.

Figure 4.6: Category shrinkage signals

Gain and loss—Horlicks	All India (Urban and Rural)	
	2020	2019
Lapse from category	845	400
Home-made	-250	-75
Cereals	-350	-125
Milk drop	-245	-200

All figures in the above chart are for illustration purposes only.

Looking at this data, one can clearly see the drop is happening on account of the increasing appeal of home-made options, cereals and even a drop in the consumption of milk which is the carrier for HFDs. Such a perplexing finding is not unusual in research, but brand managers have to apply their ingenuity or conduct additional research/dipsticks to take corrective action.

In this case, the problem was further sliced to understand the age of consumers who were impacted, and if they were satisfied with the new product or line extension launch (specific to older consumers), as also increasing media weight in geographies where cereals like Kellogg's were gaining some traction.

In addition to the above, more fundamental work was done to develop the new creative copy of Horlicks to reinstate the critical need of nutrition to draw consumers back into the fold, as will be explained later.

Slowdown

The situation gets only more uphill from here because it's often difficult to establish what constitutes slowdown. If you are growing, but not fast enough, the ancillary question is, relative to what else? Below is a figure that illustrates how best to understand what real slowdown is, since the solution will depend on that.

Figure 4.7: Growth rings

The growth rates for respective brands usually have to be more than the growth rates from the outermost onion ring. For instance, if the GDP growth rate is 5 per cent and FMCG is 8 per cent, it's okay to expect category growth and brand growth a few points above that but the converse is not true. If the FMCG growth rates, especially pertinent to food and beverage for a brand like Horlicks, is in low single digits like 4 per cent, then expecting the brand to do 10 per cent may be unrealistic.

However, companies are driven by internal logic and that has merit as long as there is recognition of the industry or sector slowdown and willingness (read as effort and resources) to invest in countervailing factors is present. The problem arises when ambition exists, indifferent to the outside world, making desirable growth rates an irrational ask.

Now, assuming you had the resources, your options of staying ahead of the growth curve of other companies or the industry or sector you belong to, will include one or many of the following:

-   Building relevance for your category, reflecting the reality of the times you live in and suggesting a better solution out of the current growth impasse. For instance, if consumers are cutting down consumption due to COVID-19, then the solution for a food manufacturer has to be around the lines of immunity and overall health to increase the attraction of its product.
-   Sharpening the functional benefit to appeal to the logical right side of the brain. If you are selling mobile phones, you clearly need to play up the advantages of your camera for selfies, videos, posts to stay ahead of the faceless others who are vying for precious consumer attention.
-   Sometimes you may have to crank up the emotional appeal of your brand. If you are selling Sprite, but during COVID-19 nobody wishes to consume a non-essential product, your brand story may have to be spun around the absolute importance of staying stress-free, when the whole world is pelting dos and don'ts of staying safe, through a modification of your campaign 'All taste, no gyaan'. A proposition that may or may not win

100 per cent support, but will definitely attract attention to the brand at a point when it could fall into oblivion.

Thus, it's important to have a good assessment of the situation before palliative or accelerating moves are made towards securing growth. Very often, managers fail to appreciate this, charging into hasty reactions educated by previous learnings or unwise counsel, failing to achieve desired results.

So now that we have a sense of diagnostics, it's very useful to get ahead in the game for fresher and more productive solutions for your brand. For this we need to go back to the consumer and place him in a Petri dish to understand what he is really up to. To make maximum impact, one needs to first know the lay of the land, where the consumer is moving day after day, to find multiple opportunities for your brand to meet and greet him or her.

Week 7 and 8

Know Your Consumer

The seventh and eighth weeks are for being noticed as a manager with some potential. You have some understanding of boss management and a modicum of self-awareness (which is a long journey, but it progresses well if you are cognizant of it), now the time has come to make some early impact. People should notice you for the right reasons because impressions, right or wrong, are being formed and you don't want to lose out the initial assessment people make of you when they are most open, and presumably objective, to assessing you. More importantly, you don't want to lose out on being assessed at all because professional oblivion is as good as failure.

Office: plan and shape your first impression

So how do you make an early impact? It's not without a reason that they say first impressions matter a lot. How you are perceived initially builds a base and people tend to usually draw other conclusions to validate that later. So, not only must you make the right impression, but you also need to reinforce it.

But what sort of impression do you make? As you are building brands, how do others see you as a brand? Many don't think about it; those who do and take measured steps stand out in the long run.

Usually, who you are for the most part: the way you act, speak and conduct yourself is absorbed by people and a gradual consensus evolves around your personality and effectiveness as a manager, in an unspoken way. If you have the right traits, you are lucky. If not, you may have to hone some and consciously exhibit them. This will give others the comfort about your leadership and professional competence to get the job done. Your managers have to trust you and you must give them enough reason for doing so.

Thus, it's very important to make an early impact, and do it the right way. It's important that you are not seen as a hustler. You need to consider the following:

- Select a few, may be one or two avenues to show your presence. Take the ones that matter from understanding your boss, as in the previous chapter. For instance, if there is a need for looking at sales in a different way, then use digital analytics to bring a fresh analysis to an old problem and add value. The multiplier on your personal brand as someone who shows initiative and works hard to understand a problem will be huge.
- Make sure your success is in keeping with the company's culture so you are seen to be contributing as a team worker not an independent loose cannon. In the early stages of your career, you are valued for your uniqueness only and only if it's within the framework that your seniors have laid out for you to operate within.
- Winning the right way is important. People will trust you on the basis of what you do. If they find your success is laudable but your methods are questionable, they will have difficulty leaving important tasks to your care. Understand the stage of the company and the brand: turnaround, start-up . . . and tailor your actions accordingly. For instance, turnarounds require swift thinking and action. Maintenance means an eye for detail and process optimization. Adapt your style accordingly rather than imposing your natural tendencies on the situation.

- Start to connect with external stakeholders and engage them to multiply your idea of success. Make them collaborators so your success builds vested interest amongst others to make it happen for all, thereby giving your success longevity and visibility from many quarters.
- Finally, use the initial projects from the point of view of how you have fared along the way and how it fills your long-term view of developing the brand. Step back and evaluate at the end how your focus was, how well you could oversee all the details or where you fell short, were the goals clear to all, did you have sufficient means and abilities on the project or were you under- or over-leveraged and finally, how did the team feel at the end— were they elevated with mutual success, or did they feel enervated or even deprived of recognition.

Take formal or informal feedback and self-assess, and get better next time. You will have to sharpen the saw of self-development a few times before variables that ensure success start to come to you more naturally. If these happen early on, the manager benefits from having an authentic style. If not, it's either late afterwards or it becomes more difficult later and managers may tend to overcompensate for their long-standing inadequacies, ending up looking unauthentic.

So now that you have made some impact and got noticed, it's time to deep-dive into the next set of developing brand competencies.

Brand competency: Know your brand

Brand managers have spent a lifetime working on the brand without knowing their consumers. Some, however, know the recipients of their brands, the consumers, like a close friend. It's very unlikely that you are successful in brand management while being an alien to your consumer. On the other hand, it's extremely probable that each step you take for your brand is visited with success because you know him or her like a member of your family.

Usage and Attitude studies become a Bible for managing brands. If it's done every few years, it can become a veritable tool for knowing your consumer. If it's not done, then you may have to do some dipstick or exploratory research and arrive at a reasonably good estimation of your consumer along the lines of the following questions that comprehensively describe the consumer.

5 Ws of a consumer

Knowing your consumer eventually entails the following five Ws asked in the context of your category and the brand.

1. Who is the consumer?
2. When is he/she interacting?
3. Where is he/she consuming?
4. What else is happening or who else is with him/her?
5. Why are they interested or not interested in the brand? Or what is their motivation or barrier?

Who is the consumer seems like an obvious query but often ends up being taken for granted so much, so often, that it misleads managers into believing that their imagination of their consumer is the reality. A big chasm exists here for several reasons. Large brands have a very diverse base of users, ranging from kids to adults, even geriatrics. This is because consumers who were wooed when they were the intended audience of the brand don't cease to consume after they have crossed the age band of consumption. Pepsi is a typical example of a brand that is consumed by all, although marketers target their brand strategy towards only the narrow age of 15 to 25. Sometimes, consumers use the brand in their own way, going beyond the intended usage of the product.

Eno, which is an antacid, is used for making fizzy drinks in hot areas like up-country Rajasthan with a concentrate like Rasna. Or as a cooking soda. This 'abuse' of the brand accounts for nearly 15 per cent of brand consumption (as per U&A studies), but little can be done to address this anomalous consumption. At other times, the brand rates so high on utility specific to a need-state that aiming towards a specific age segment makes little sense. Iodex and Vicks are the classic examples of brands which are used by all suffering from muscle pain and cold, even though the communication addresses mostly the women and kids in the household.

You might think that such research is unactionable since it's likely to throw results which are even downright embarrassing. Yet, you need to know. Turning your back on reality never helps; less so in marketing where knowing is the first step to strategizing right.

So, how do you determine the profile of your consumers? Whatever the brand, you need to start with your existing users (those targeted by the brand) and profile them with respect to:

1. How often they are consuming in terms of count of occasions of consumption.
2. How much they are consuming in each single act of consumption.

The mistake very often made is estimating the frequency of consumption or point 1 above, but not the depth or weight of consumption or point 2. This leads to an erroneous understanding of the consumer profile since you want to not just know who is consuming, but also how much. If you get the two, then you multiply one with the other and you have a total weight of the consumption. The data should be so granular and so simple in the same breath that it can almost be visualized.

For instance, if the consumption of milk in this country was one big glass of milk, then intuitively what you want to know is how this breaks into consumption for each age segment, rather than merely knowing how everyone is consuming it. In other words, you want to know not only how many in percentage terms (or the incidence of consumption), but also how much they are consuming (or the depth of consumption) so you get to know the total amount (or weight) of consumption which can help you break up a glass of milk amongst its constituent segment of consumers.

This difference is critical and needs to be understood in detail.

So, if we ask in a quantitative research across a significant number of households across the country, representative of the population, who consumes milk in the house, we may get data as below, which is quite inconclusive. In the figure below, we have a break-up of population in million (mio.) in India, against which we put the percentage of people who have answered 'yes' for the question 'who consumes milk in your household'. This question is multiple coding; hence, in the same household, many people will consume milk and the percentage in column three will not add up. After this, we multiply the population with the percentage of population in that age bracket and arrive at the actual number of people in millions consuming milk, totalling 628 million in urban India. Finally, when you divide the number of consumers in each segment by the total number of consumers, you get the 'incidence of consumption' in percentage. Now, if all of urban India's consumption of milk was represented by a single glass of milk, then about 57 per cent of that glass of milk is drunk by people less than 30 years, as per column 4.

Figure 5.1: Incidence of consumption of milk

Age	Population (mio.)	Consuming milk (%)	Consuming milk (mio.)	Incidence of consumption (%)
0–8	200	80%	160	25%
15–30	400	50%	200	32%
31–45	350	30%	105	17%
46–60	250	25%	62.5	10%
Above 60	200	50%	100	16%
Total	1400		628	100%

All figures in the above chart are for illustration purposes only.

Now, referring to Figure 5.2 below, if we supplement this question with how often they are consuming milk (or the frequency of consumption as in column 3); and how much in each consumption occasion (or depth of consumption measured in 150 ml cup or 200 ml glass or 250 ml large glass available in the households and then summed up for the total population), we can break up the national glass of milk by multiplying the two data columns to arrive at the total litres consumed (or weight of consumption) as per the shaded last column. From this you would infer that about 79 per cent of the consumption of milk is accounted for by people below thirty years of age. A vastly different picture is obtained from the one above by merely researching from two different perspectives: frequency and depth of consumption, on multiplying which we get the total weight of consumption.

Which is the better picture? Clearly the total weight of consumption than the mere incidence of consumption. Hence, the question of who the consumer is should be quantified with the above qualifiers to arrive at the true picture.

Figure 5.2: Frequency, depth and weight of consumption

Age	Consuming milk (mio.)	Frequency of consumption	Depth of consumption (ml)	Weight of consumption (litre)	Weight of consumption (%)
0–8	160	3	300	144	40%
15–30	200	2	350	140	39%
31–45	105	1.6	250	42	12%
46–60	62.5	1.3	150	12	3%
Above 60	100	1.1	200	22	6%
Total	628			360	100%

All figures in the above chart are for illustration purposes only.

We will answer the question of who the consumer is using a few other criteria such as psychographics (segmentation of consumers based on mental archetypes), but before that, let's understand the other Ws.

When is he/she interacting with the category?

Now that we have pried into the household, understanding who is consuming what, it's time to ask 'When?' For another category (taking a transverse look at different categories), we can slice this question by day parts. So you could have Horlicks during breakfast, post-lunch, evening snack, post-dinner. This kind of data becomes very useful when it's compared over two time periods as in the case below from a 2014 and 2019 U&A study.

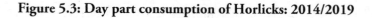

Figure 5.3: Day part consumption of Horlicks: 2014/2019

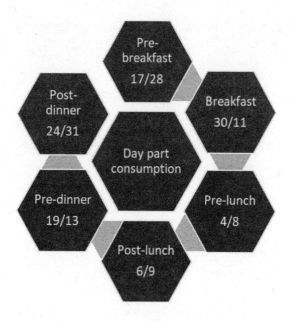

All figures in the above chart are for illustration purposes only.

The figures above indicate the consumption percentage in each time band with respect to years 2014 and 2019. As can be seen from the figures above, the consumption of Horlicks has increased in the pre-breakfast, pre-lunch, post-lunch and post-dinner occasions but decreased in breakfast and pre-dinner consumption occasions. Losing out in breakfast occasion would be of critical concern since Horlicks holds a stranglehold position in this occasion with its importance on providing day-long nutrition to children. Likewise, the pre-dinner or late evening occasion is critical for kids returning from play or tuitions and must be grown for the brand to retain its relevance in this critical day part.

Where is the consumer indulging? In a different analysis for Lay's chips, the following occasions for the brand were found, but unlike

Horlicks, this spanned both in home and out of home moments. Here, it was sufficient to know what Lay's naturally associates best with or where it can be potentially associated to drive its consumption in the initial years of the category establishment.

Figure 5.4: Lay's consumption occasions

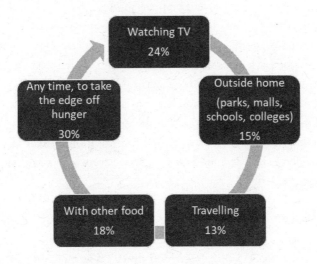

All figures in the above chart are for illustration purposes only.

Research with kids and teens revealed different percentages for each of these segments and a communication and promotion plan was drawn up to address consumers for each segment. A special TV campaign was made with Ranbir Kapoor cueing chipping as an essential part of watching TV, much like popcorn has been built around movie-viewing. A special travel pack was launched at railways and airports to build appeal specifically for this occasion. Such studies are priceless, therefore, in building fresh or even reinforcing the brand's consumption opportunities. If done well, it can even help in expanding the target audience to the entire family as, for instance, when they are eating out by planting appetizing food lenticulars (backlit 3D visuals) in restaurants cueing Lay's as an accompaniment with burgers or pizza.

What else is happening around him/her is the next question to address about our consumers as we delve deeper in their life.

In the case of Lay's, the above research revealed accidentally (it was not a part of the research) that consumers loved to have a dip with their chips. A dip could be plain tomato sauce, or a salsa sauce, or even a fancy dip made of cheese and yoghurt. None of these were in the product domain of the brand. However, a special promotion was designed wherein sachets of dips were offered to consumers, communicated through a high-octane chip-n-dip campaign with associated youth imagery to bolster Lay's overall brand image.

An extensive observation study to understand what else is happening in youths' life around the consumption of their favourite brand, Pepsi, revealed the following associations, creating tangibles to intangible cues:

- Product
    o Is the ultimate thirst quencher with a taste spin
    o Tastes best with spicy food though Thums-Up had a slight advantage in north India with older males
    o Gets spiced up with a pinch of salt or even a dash of lemon amongst die-hard Pepsi fans
    o Its slight sweetness was preferred over Coke
    o The dark colour of cola imparts a mystique to the brand over its competitors' products—Sprite, Fanta, Gold Spot
    o Is the preferred drink over sports drinks even now since it is seen to be energizing. However, Red Bull is gaining increasing traction in this space

- Accompaniments
    o Pepsi is a perfect accompaniment on an outing with friends
    o 500 ml Pepsi PET is a great way to recharge

- o No party is complete without a bag of Lay's and Pepsi—it's an uber cool combo
- o Is a great treat when I am by myself, with fast food like pizza when studying at night
- o Invokes as much fun as alcohol without losing control

- Imagery
  - o Is really cool to be with
  - o Becomes a badge of my identity when I have a Pepsi can—I feel confident
  - o It stands for doing what I like notwithstanding popular opinion—Let's me be me as I am
  - o Unlike other drinks, it's contemporary and with the times, even ahead of it by anticipating trends and being in sync with it
  - o It's the choice of the new generation of achievers and celebrities who forge their own destiny
  - o The sweating bottle of Pepsi with those dew drops is a life-saver on a scorching day after gruelling work

As you can see from the above statements from Pepsi's primary target audience, the youth, the brand lends itself to associations across many usage occasions, even unexpected ones. In fact, in personification studies on the brand, it is likened to a tiger or a cheetah (swift and agile), Formula One driver (competitive), eagle (soaring above the rest) and smartphone (intelligent and futuristic).

All these associations are enviable ammunition in the arsenal of a brand manager who can deploy this to extend (among non-users), remind (among users) and deepen (among loyalists and evangelists) the brand's power ever increasingly. Without the knowledge of these, you would be knocking at the wrong doors or worse still, missing out on calling your fans for your support even when they are all too willing to stand in for you.

Why are they interested or indifferent or even repulsed by your brand or category is the other big question that needs to be unravelled in the brand manager's diary of her consumers. This is also referred to as the 'barrier and motivation' study. In a study done for Bausch and Lomb contact lenses, the following reasons were adduced by consumers in favour of adopting the category:

-   Good looks: distinctly enhances your visual appeal in the eyes of the opposite sex
-   Sports: conventional glasses drop off the face hindering full movement
-   Inconvenience: spectacles fog, require maintenance and are seen to be tacky and sloppy

The reasons for not adopting, on the contrary, are:

-   Price: prohibitive entry cost and ongoing maintenance cost, including the cost of the lens care fluid solutions. And since lenses have to be had in addition to the glasses (they are not seen to replace glasses) this is a pure additional cost.
-   Bothersome: wearing them every day is an elaborate ritual of taking off, cleaning up and maintaining them. Disposables reduce the problem but don't eliminate it, apart from the fact that they are expensive. Hence, sustained usage is a challenge even if people embrace the category initially. It's also seen to be intrusive, requiring to be placed inside the eye—not being able to sleep with lenses on, or washing your eyes against dust and other contaminants calls for extra care which can be quite irksome.

Hence, lenses have had mixed success with users in spite of India's rampant eye problems. And the category has a skew towards females over males owing to the elaborate use and maintenance ritual.

It's important to note that unlike almost all the other researches, the barrier and motivation study is done amongst light users and non-users. Often, such studies are ignored as managers get caught up overanalysing their existing users to woo them, ignoring the opportunity to draw those outside into their brand's fold.

It's not often that brands will have most or all of these studies available for inquisitive brand managers to pore over to reach their solutions. In such a case, a few dipstick studies or a small digital quantitative study should be organized. Not knowing your users would otherwise seriously undermine the chances for a brand to expand its user base.

Now that we have some understanding of the consumer, let's take a deep-dive and see if we can typify him/her so better solutions can be designed to address their need.

Consumer typology

To understand consumers in their entirety, it's customary to study them as human beings with a focus on their view on life, on parenting, on food and beverage consumption, and only after lensing them through all these, is their attitude towards the category of HFD taken.

When you club the following statements of consumers towards various aspects, you get a rough image of the person. Often these are captured by descriptors that help one get an instant recognition of the type of person. Such descriptors are called consumer typology.

Below are the archetypes of consumers explained with respect to the HFD category relevant for our analysis.

Self-starters:

    a.   Attitude towards life
        i.   I like to stay ahead in life, thinking ahead, planning ahead.

ii. I consider the pros and cons of a topic so I can make my own decisions and not be led blindly by others.

iii. I want to be in a better place in the future than the one I am in today.

iv. For this, I am willing to make all the effort and I am often willing to go the extra mile for it.

b. Attitude towards parenting

i. I enjoy being the parent of my child, it's the best thing in my life.

ii. I wish the best for my child and am willing to invest as much as is required for doing so.

iii. I push my kids to become achievers in life and work along with them in their studies and extra-curriculars.

iv. However, I emphasize more on their studies than anything else.

c. Attitude towards health and well-being

i. I believe what you eat is what you become.

ii. I read the labels and make sure only the best goes into my child.

iii. Food supported with science is desirable, even health supplements are welcome.

iv. I am willing to experiment with new things to achieve the best nutrition for my child.

d. Attitude towards HFD

i. I prefer the HFD made at home than the ones I buy.

ii. I don't find the HFDs satiating, I prefer the more traditional options.

In sum, Self-starters are organized, ambitious and well-planned, so that they are able to get the best for their child.

Nourishers

a. Attitude towards life

      i.   My family is more important than me.

      ii. Taking care of my family is my first priority.

      iii. I am very sociable and prefer to be in the company of others.

b. Attitude towards parenting

      i.   Raising kids is the most fun thing.

      ii. I want them to be successful and act like their friend to help them grow along.

c. Attitude towards health and well-being

      i.   Healthy people achieve more in life.

      ii. Good health is more important than anything else and it means not falling sick or recovering quickly even if you do.

      iii. Home-made food is the best option for my family.

d. Attitude towards HFD

      i.   I don't trust what's written on the labels.

      ii. It's too expensive.

      iii. It does not mix well with water.

In sum, Nourishers are family-oriented people looking for holistic traditional nutrition for their family.

Relaxed

a. Attitude towards life

      i.   I live for today, not worrying too much about tomorrow since I can't control it.

      ii. I wish to reduce the stress of life, so I can live to the maximum every day.

      iii. I like to keep things simple, so I can do more in a day without getting caught up in unnecessary complications.

b. Attitude towards parenting

      i.   I find parenting very stressful.

      ii.   Other parents can call me laid-back but I tend to be relaxed about it to avoid getting worked up. I want them to pursue extra-curriculars and not just be focused on studies.

      iii. I teach my kids to be independent so they can manage their life, and I, my own.

  c. Attitude towards health and well-being

      i.   I don't like to stress too much over food.

      ii.   I can eat the same things many times, keeping life simple.

      iii. I don't read too much of the labels and like superfoods and supplements because they give dense nutrition with least fuss.

  d. Attitude towards HFD

      i.   I don't like HFD—it's not filling enough.

      ii.   It has too many calories and is meant for children and geriatrics, not for me.

In essence, Relaxed are organized, ambitious and well-planned, so that they are able to get the best for their child.

Innovators

  a. Attitude towards life

      i.   I like to stand out in the crowd, refusing to blend in.

      ii.   I make my choices about my life carefully to be distinct from others.

      iii. I follow the latest trends to be in sync with the current times.

  b. Attitude towards parenting

      i.   I wish I had more time for the kids.

      ii.   I would like my kids to be independent early and am confident that like me, they too can make their life-choices.

      iii. I want them to do well in studies, more than extra-curriculars.

  c. Attitude towards health and well-being

      i. I believe that health is the basis of everything and I place a lot of importance on meals.

      ii. I make my own judgements about food, reading up whatever is available on the subject while keeping abreast with the latest in health and nutrition.

  d. Attitude towards HFD

      i. I like HFD, the taste or the nutrition they claim to contain makes a sufficient meal.

      ii. I believe that home-made food is sufficient but don't have the time or knowledge to always provide the same to my child.

Innovators are interested in their outer image and do everything possible inside the home to come out best when they step out.

Seekers

  a. Attitude towards life

      i. I live only once so I should live to the fullest.

      ii. Experiencing pleasure is an important part of my life.

  b. Attitude towards parenting

      i. I am concerned my kids are not active enough.

      ii. I try and give my kids experiences of various kinds so they can explore the best in their life.

      iii. I wish them to be independent early on.

  c. Attitude towards health and well-being

      i. Eating healthy comes naturally to me.

      ii. As long as I look after daily health, I will be okay in the long term.

      iii. I eat mostly what I want.

    d. Attitude towards HFD
        i. I am tired of the limited options in HFD.
        ii. I wish to get more nutrition than the current range of
           HFDs is offering.

Therefore, Seekers want to make the most of life, wishing to give their kids maximum exposure in a natural, healthy way and for them, HFDs have limited appeal.

By looking at the quantitative data around this research (the recruitment questionnaire, and their indexing on attitude statements), we can quantify these consumer typologies, allotting a distinct weight to each type. The SEC classification in the table below refers to socio-economic classes in the population, ranked from A to E based on education, occupation and ownership of some household items, and regions N-W-E-S pertains to North-West-East-South parts of the country.

Figure 5.5: Consumer typology traits

Consumer typology/traits (per cent)	Self-starters	Nourishers	Relaxed	Innovators	Seekers
Representation	25	17	18	15	25
SEC A–B/C–D ratio	46/51	40/57	50/49	53/47	70/30
Regional skew N-W-E-S ratio	49/51	46/54	55/45	52/48	40/60

All figures in the above chart are for illustration purposes only.

Thus, we can see that we have five distinct sets of consumers who are sufficiently different to be cast in various moulds, even though they exhibit some common features. Making this sort of distinction, as we will see later also, helps us communicate with a sharp focus with our consumers to build affinity towards the brand.

Having understood the consumer typologies, we need to now look at the need-states in more detail. Needs as we have seen before are broadly stated and they can't be converted into demand if we don't slice them up into various sub-types contextualized within the consumer's mindset. For instance, a consumer may be feeling down and may want his spirits uplifted. This could lead to the consumption of any of these categories: movie-going, listening to music, shopping, drinking, eating out. Fine-tuning need-states into specific wants and removing barriers or giving new benefits creates a demand for our brand, as we have seen in the NWB/BD framework. Now we slice demand into specific and compelling demand moments.

From another qualitative research on food categories, the following need-states were found:

- **Sustenance**: Enough nutrition to get by in the day. Often this takes the shape of food that is full of energy, offers basic nutrition and scores high on value. Categories like biscuits and staples feature here, which pack enough carbohydrates (in some cases simple carbohydrates like glucose) to give high calories. This need usually expresses itself highly during mealtimes when the need is to fill up and satisfy hunger as well.
- **Indulgence**: Food that really scores high on taste delight. What consumers are seeking is a real fun and enjoyable experience that also uplifts their mood. Nutrition may take a back seat here and often sinfulness of excessive or unhealthy ingredients becomes permissive in this need-state. The associated feelings of reward and celebration are common when categories like chocolates and fast food are considered.
- **Nourishment**: The overall sense of filling up the body with essential nutrients to keep it going sustainably. Building up

for the future or enhancing the body's capabilities for bigger challenges are important to this mindset. Consumers are willing to pay a premium, sacrifice some taste and even form a habit of it to ensure continuous replenishment of nutrition in their daily lives. The associated codes are less around fun, more around responsibility and well-being. HFD, milk products, even if they are seen to be boring, index high here.

- **Growth**: This is a specific need with clear growth markers. Consumers seek return here much as they seek return on investment in stocks. 'How tall, how big, how strong, how disease or illness-free' will a consumer of a category of health drinks and foods be: such anxieties have to be answered clearly because consumers are seeking quantifiable results that can be calibrated over time with disciplined investment of time and money. Science and measurement are critical determinants in this sphere of need-state.

- **Convalescence**: A smaller set of consumers but with high loyalty and high usage are those seeking to restore their life to what it was before they fell sick. Suffering from 'sub-health' (neither unhealthy enough to be sick, nor healthy enough to be operating at full efficiency), which undermines their appreciation of life, they will go to any extent to feel better. Brands that help consumers with overall well-being through routine nourishment like those offered by Dabur or Himalaya qualify in this category. The demand is high, and believability and loyalty is no less, if products offer superior performance. The audience for this segment tend to be more from older age groups.

Now if you intersect the above need-states with the occasion of consumption, you end up with many demand-moments as below:

Figure 5.6: Day-part to Need-state table

Day-part/ Need-state	Sustenance (15%)	Indulgence (22%)	Nourishment (30%)	Growth (18%)	Convalescence (15%)
Morning	Quick breakfast	Delicious start	Healthy start	Protein loading	Body upkeep
Pre-lunch	Hunger buster	Appetizer	Essential nutrition	Extra growth	Repair food
Post-lunch	Light fill	Tasty break	Quality energy	On the go nutrition	Light refills
Post-dinner	Final fill	Mood uplifter	Vitality	Growth enhancers	Body build

All figures in the above chart are for illustration purposes only.

Behavioural psychology tells us that we can be in different need-states at different times. Hence, it's not necessary that the same person will exhibit a standard, unchanging inclination. At one moment, he may be in a nourishing mindset and at another moment, he could be thinking of growth. Thus, instead of a consumer conforming to a single need-state or a typology, he or she proliferates with a presence across many moments of varied demands. These are the 'demand moments' which, if optimally captured, will yield to conversion or purchase in favour of the brand. When we cross-tabulate consumer typology with need-states we get the following demand-moments:

Figure 5.7: Demand-moments

Typology/ Need-state	Sustenance	Indulgence	Nourishment	Growth	Convalescence
Self-starters	Quick fill	Taste blast	Positive nutrition	Physical, mental growth	Fast recovery
Nourishers	Long lasting energy	Family fun	Responsible nutrition	Overall growth	Long lasting well-being
Relaxed	All day energy	Balancing life	Holistic nutrition	Growth enablers	Managing the day
Innovators	Ample energy	Better taste	Staying ahead	Distinctive growth	Leading change
Seekers	Always exploring	Newer options	Enhancing capability	Enabling growth	Creating new possibilities

Brand managers will have to make choices as to which segment they want to occupy. For instance, Horlicks has decided to play in the space of Growth and Nourishment primarily even though it also plays in the Convalescence space and is not indifferent to Indulgence either, given its trademark taste that consumers love. But brand management is about making choices and staying sharp on course (more in the next chapter).

The advantage of plotting demand-moments as above is that it allows marketers to have a more meaningful conversation with consumers who are seen with respect to a specific state of mind, not through an aggregated assumption of their mindset. Invariably, this tailored approach helps creates more resonance with consumers.

Connecting back to what we said about NWB/BD cycle, we are underlaying another layer below this: the AIDA model or Awareness-Interest-Decision-Action which wedges your brand and not the competitor's between want and demand. Except we add two more units in this making it **AIPAR**, where P stands for *Pre-disposition* and R stands for *Reaction*. Predisposition refers to the demand-moments when a consumer of a specific type is in a specific need-state providing an opportunity for a customized, tailored communication when he or she is most prone to listening. Reaction pertains to the post-consumption experience of the consumer and sharing with others that drives not only her repurchase but the purchase of her peers. In digital marketing, reaction has become very critical in influencing purchase of other consumers who haven't bought the product but want to know, through ratings and comments, from the experience of those who have. We will explore these in more detail in Integrated Marketing later.

Now that we have understood the consumer somewhat, let's go fishing again in the market to understand the category we are playing in, both from the inside and outside and target the ones that make maximum strategic sense for us.

Week 9

How Do I Segment and Target Him/Her?

We talked about Specialist as an attribute that brand managers need to aspire to in building their functional skill. Most brand managers will need outside help since they are subject-matter experts only in a few areas and often not in the products they are working on. While you can take external help in this, it's extremely useful to develop the traits of a specialist which you can exercise at will, should the situation demand.

Managerial skill: Specialist

Specialists are driven by the zeal to probe every query that pertains to their subject matter. They will evaluate a specialist topic from various perspectives, showing a lot of ingenuity in approach and enterprise, to answer far and wide. In doing so, they return with gems of information that give team members a distinct advantage on the matter in question.

Our recommendation would be to take one area that interests you, even if it's somewhat rudimentary and start mining the details when you get some time off (we will explore making time for yourself later). For instance, if you are working on food and various tastes interest you, then read up whatever you can lay your hands on without an agenda: the physiology of the tongue that perceives tastes, the cerebral involvement in recognition and appreciation of taste, the fundamental flavours, combination of flavours, how texture and bite impacts taste, what are the various ingredients used in the food industry and so on.

Not only will you develop a genuine interest in your project at a fundamental level which is bound to win respect from your team members, but your work will become far more differentiated and meaningful. Gradually, this ability to scan the minutest of details will expand to other areas as your eye for detail improves, which will not fail to make you a formidable professional. We have seen outstanding performers amongst our seniors often exhibit this virtue. Over time, you will be able to probe in detail even on a subject that is not of your interest—a virtue that will stand you in good stead in a leadership role as well. It's also time to look at the next soft skill as you are truly getting immersed in your job now.

Office art: understanding and leveraging company culture

Having negotiated your success parameters with the boss and secured some early impact, you should be in a position to judge the company culture. There is no hard and fast formula for this save some intuitive understanding based on what you observe. Look at these indicators. Are meetings done in a formal way to inform everyone or do issues get picked and discussed openly? When it comes to getting work done, what is valued more: doing it on time or adhering to the process? How do people get work done? Do they appeal to a single influencer or is authority spread and more democratic? What are the ways used to align people— formally through meetings, or closed-door one-to-one meetings? Do people talk about conflicts openly or do they avoid them? Does the company reward star performers or is it more inclined to looking at team workers? And finally, does the organization have well-defined values that show through consistently or is it a miasma of opportunism and convenience?

You will have to sharpen your senses to understand these things. To get a holistic view, step out and check with your customers, suppliers, distributors, outside analysts, R&D people and even ex-employees from various departments who carry the history of the organization in their vibrant memories. Sometimes, what misses an internal eye is very perceptible to outside forces and hence, it's important to do a full 360-degree scan to ascertain your company's culture, keeping in mind other companies in the same industry or even outside.

To enrich your perspective of the company at a holistic level, it's useful to hold little conversations with people inside and outside the company. While you need to be professional in the way you conduct these, be conscious that you are also building powerful bridges for future conversations and cross-alliances. However, to start right, don't jump to informality but build a rapport. Ask them questions on the challenges the organization is facing, what's impeding it, where are the debottlenecking opportunities in their view. Keeping similar questions, you can measure up the answers and get a perspective on people's internal complexion: optimist, inveterate pessimist, opportunists, creative–innovative, indifferent. This is of huge value when you go ahead making future cross-alliances, which we will examine in the next chapter. But before that, let's understand how to slice and dice consumers for an effective marketing strategy to sharpen our core: brand competence.

Segmentation and targeting: meaning and scope

Segmentation has expanded in its usage considerably in the last few years. It's used loosely for any visible cluster that reflects a pattern amenable for commercial exploitation. Let's evaluate the critical ones that will help us sharpen our strategic insight.

Category segmentation: The first segment that we look at, almost reflexively, is the Category segmentation. It pertains to the category that is described by consumers as a class of products that fall broadly under one kind of usage. So for Maggi, it's noodles; for Horlicks, it's the category of Health Food Drinks; for Sensodyne, it's toothpaste and for Hush Puppies, it's shoes.

It's the closest to what consumers think first and within which they situate the brands. Brand managers should claim as many category benefits as possible and also differentiate with other brands in the category to get maximum share of the category pie.

Category segmentation helps brand managers cue the broad benefits of that category in the least time. Even 7Up, which segmented the market as 'The Uncola', had to refer to Cola to give its brand idea a known reference. Then it proceeded to differentiate. On the other hand, scores of brands have failed because of their inability to identify themselves with respect to the category consumers commonly refer to.

After understanding clearly the *immediate category* they are operating in, brand managers should step out and look at the next layer of competition where they can source more business from. These are being broken up into *proximal category, related category, distant category segments.* Usually, brand managers get stuck at the immediate category level, reinforced by the market share conversation in the company driven by competitive pressures. However, looking beyond the immediate segments is not only the inspiration for future growth but also insurance of steady cash flow. Below is the onion ring of segments that brand managers need to develop a keen eye for, early in their career.

Figure 6.1: Category onion rings

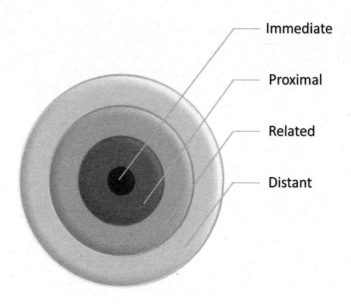

For most, this becomes a blind spot once they join a business even though this makes a lot of sense when you seek new markets for higher growth in each market, as each segment has its distinctive codes that need to be unlocked to tap growth. And this starts with knowing these segments. So below is a list of this category segmentation supported by examples to widen our lens of competition.

Figure 6.2: Category segmentation examples

Brand/ Category segment	Immediate	Proximal	Related	Distant
Horlicks	Pediasure, Bournvita, Complan	Milk, cereals	Juices	Dosa, upma
Sunfeast noodles	Top Ramen noodles	Chips, namkeen, chocolates	Pasta, pizza	Samosa, vada, roti-daal
Surf	Ariel	Tide	Washing powder, washing bar	Washerman, dry cleaning
Parachute	Cocoraj (coconut oil)	Bhringraj oil (other ayurvedic oils for hair)	Conditioner	Hair parlour

As can be seen from the above grid, most of the time the interbrand warfare keeps managers busy, with mutual wars that can actually undermine the value of the category in the long term. Yet, in reality, opportunities can be explored in proximal, related and distant categories and alternatives can unfold. As Horlicks did when it tagged itself to milk, which it would quite often lose to, by maintaining that it increases the power of milk by supplementing it with added nutrients not naturally found, captured in the idea '*Horlicks badaye doodh ki shakti*'. Or while noodle players are sparring for a market share below Maggi noodles, the leader, they could start targeting the occasions when light Indian snacks are consumed at four o'clock in the evening and bring out the benefits of their proposition. While they would have to build credibility with this story with some innovation and science, the potential of such an idea to disrupt the category is huge. Or while Parachute is trying to gain market share from Cocoraj, it might find a decline in urban markets because a start-up like Urban Company has made home grooming so easy and cheap that nobody oils and washes their hair any more. If they foresee this threat coming, then they can venture into the 'service' aspect of this business with Parachute home grooming and protect their brand. Thus, keeping the proximal, related and distant categories in sight can yield hugely beneficial opportunities for growth.

Demographic segmentation based on age, education and occupation of an individual—the erstwhile SEC or NCCS (New Consumer Classification System based on the education of the chief wage earner and the list of consumer durables owned by the household which captures the affordability quotient, valid for both urban and rural India that BARC has now instituted)—outlines the consumer with physical coordinates, which is the basis for media planning and distribution strategy as this data can be overlaid over town class (classified as metros and further basis population strata of 5 million, 1 million, less than a million, going all the way to villages with a population of 50,000 people). Since most government surveys and NRS (National Readership Survey) are linked to demographics, this segmentation is absolutely necessary for executing all your marketing plans.

Psychographic segmentation tends to get specific to the category and while you can manage without it and run a very basic marketing plan, not doing this would severely handicap every marketing discussion. As discussed before, consumers need to be cast in typology basis their attitude towards category proximally, and life in a distant way. Intersecting this with need-states becomes critical to getting a robust understanding of the consumer who otherwise stays as a lumpy mass, defying your attempt to influence their behaviour.

Behavioural segmentation has become critical in the digital age. Data analytics and shopper understanding studies (done on consumers in shopping mode at the retail point, especially organized trade, where they navigate aisles and pick-n-choose) are seminal to catch the consumer when he is buying other categories while evaluating yours. This gives priceless insights on how to wean them towards your aisle by laying appropriate allurements in his path of purchase.

For instance, a buyer of diapers and baby personal care products is a very likely buyer of milk, kid snacks, prams and so on. By collaborating with an e-commerce or an organized partner, you can plan to intersect the consumer when she is buying any of these items. This works in both offline and online environments and is far more effective than bombarding your TV advertisements to all hoping you get to the right audience.

Micro-segmentation: The intrusion of digital in our lives makes for a whole new opportunity based on the definite stage of the consumer's mindset, as he moves close to the brand. This ensures closing all the gaps in the last mile to ensure purchase, something which was unimaginable a few years ago. Thus, you have consumers who are segmented further as: aware but not interested in the category, interested but not certain, certain but not buying, buying but not consuming, consuming and ready to share their experience through reviews. For each of these states, content has to be curated to elicit the desired reaction. This will be described in more detail in the section on Integrated Marketing covering Digital Marketing.

So, we have a few segmentation areas. Often, many are not used or joined together for a complete consumer profiling. Below is a list that you must absolutely master for leading marketing decisions further downstream.

Figure 6.3: Segmentation type, applicability, measurement

Segmentation	Category	Demographic	Psychographic	Behavioural	Micro
Used for	Market share, innovation	Distribution strategy, media planning	Communication, positioning, targeting innovation	Shopper insight, retail strategy	Digital content, microtargeting
Outcome/ measurement	Share gain	Distribution gain, share of voice	Brand equity scores, communication recall, new products adoption	Share gain, forward stock share	Higher conversion, Positive reviews, brand endorsement

The above table shows the segmentation that one needs to know for various purposes and the resultant outcome to measure its efficacy. Things like share of voice (percentage of total media noise of the brand measured in GRPs over that of the category GRPs) and forward stock share (visibility of a brand divided by the total visibility of the category measured basis pack facings in retail, in percentage) can be used following the segmentation approach to reduce waste and uncover growth opportunities for the brand.

Targeting: the art of making choices

In marketing, you are tempted to do everything. It's too difficult to let go of an opportunity, however small it is. Yet good decisions are as much about taking the right step as dodging the ones that are potentially harmful. How do you decide where the resources and time of a company are best spent on growing a brand? Here is a matrix to help you harness the uncertainty.

Figure 6.4: OFEM grid

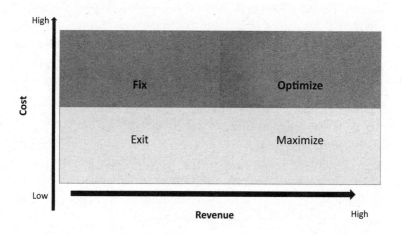

As can be seen from the figure above, targeting or choosing what segment matters most can be done by optimizing the return on investment measured by evaluating the Revenue earned as a result of the Cost incurred through time, resources and cash. We saw earlier the various uses of segmentation for executing marketing decisions on-ground. Here is a look at which of these aspects can be judged across the spectrum of choice through the lens of targeting. We call this the OFEM choice grid, standing for Optimize-Fix-Exit-Maximize choices that this evaluation will entail.

Optimize: This is the area of high cost and high revenue. It's valuable since it accounts for a lot of revenue for brands. But for various reasons, this segment is expensive to address causing the brand P&L to bleed. From the above grid of segmentation choices, you may have varied opportunities to optimize in segments in Figure 6.3 above. For category segmentation, if you are gaining share but spending a lot, look at cheaper media options to reach consumers, and find more cost-effective communication and engagement opportunities.

From a demographic perspective, do an analysis of your consumers and see which segment costs more to reach and convert. The ones in top metros or those in 10 lakh towns and through numeric outlets or weighted ones. Again, which is more cost-effective to reach—the ones that are richer or those lower down, who show more loyalty. From a psychographic perspective, find which consumers are showing a better conversion when you target them on social media, search, etc., and see how you can leverage more of these before you go to the more expensive options. From a behavioural and microsegment perspective, where do you need to push the button harder in their purchase cycle: when they are evaluating you with other related categories but not buying, and how do you do so—with more promotions, and more bundled deals or just sharper communication?

Optimizing is a critical vector that needs to be leveraged for now and later. If you ignore it for cost reasons, your growth is very likely to be challenged. Usually optimization offers huge *operational savings* in various ways.

Fix: These are strange animals, they cost a lot of resources and money but yield relatively little returns, at least in the short term. Typically, new products fall in this regime, which require a certain amount of volume of business before scale is built for healthy returns to follow. If there is consensus in the company that in this segment you are catering to a specific need and a specific consumer even though the initial costs are high, then by all means *invest and grow*, keeping a tight review of costs versus returns. Typically, these tend to be of strategic interest where the company sees a positive outlook further on the horizon.

Exit: These need to be identified, if they are not known, through a search of what is called value-destroyers, namely brands that don't give much revenue but drain the resources of the company, compromising its overall efficiency and preventing the deployment of the full might of the organization towards focused brands.

If they are known and not acted upon, then brand managers should have the courage to stand up and call them out to management's attention. Growth as a way to grow is appreciated by all for managers but as organizations mature, there will also be appreciation of prudent exit calls on exiting businesses that don't give much.

Maximize: This is the cash bag of the company. A perfect intersection of great proposition, assiduously cultivated and consistently maintained. This is the spine of any business and brands that lie in this area need to be looked after with great care.

Whatever it takes to keep them going must be maintained— growing share in the existing category or even from the proximal one, maximizing distribution and communication and engagement with chosen consumers with the right demographics and last-mile influencing so that the psychographic, behavioural and micro-segmentation variables work well.

But after doing all this, you will be left with savings if you have done your job well. This is the result of knowing this segment well and having maximized its returns with scale and superior knowledge. Please take out these savings unabashedly and invest in other quadrants for future growth. However, two points of caution here.

- First, if you don't take the extra they generate, you would potentially short-change the future of other businesses because they generate synergies of production, logistics, manpower and distribution that can be leveraged by other brands in the portfolio.
- Second, the balance has to be just right. If you squeeze too many resources out of this segment at the cost of new ideas (yes, they cross-subsidize a great deal), then you kill the goose that lays the golden eggs. Hence, care should be taken that the extra bottom line they generate should be taken out only and only if the required metrics of this segment (in terms of consumer

reach in media terms, numeric and weighted reach, production savings, etc.) are not compromised. If you don't do that with good rigour, then you grow the new business at the cost of one that is doing well.

Clever brand managers learn this skill early on. They know which brands in their portfolio can be milked and which need to be invested in.

By keeping a good mix of the first and second factor, you can spawn successes. Without it, your growth engine can splutter. Most companies have a cash cow that they leverage to grow in the future, while safeguarding today.

Below is a grid to identify segments that give early signals of targeting for OFEM evaluation so corrective measures can be put in place.

Figure 6.5: OFEM metrics

Metrics	Optimize	Fix	Exit	Maximize
Consumer	Middling recall, brand equity	Increasing/ Decreasing brand equity scores	Low recall	High brand equity scores
Distribution	Limited	High numeric, low weighted or low numeric, high weighted	Dropping availability	Wide and increasing numeric, weighted distribution
Finance	Low margins	High margins	Low margins	High margins
Operations	High fixed and variable expense	High cost	Highly inefficient	Low fixed, reducing variable due to scale

Target penetration or frequency?

A frequently asked question in marketing is whether to target penetration or frequency for an identified segment. There is usually no blanket answer for this, but a few salient points can be called out to guide this choice better.

Penetration strategy implies reaching more and more people, constantly bringing more users to the brand's fold. Frequency strategy, on the other hand, means increasing consumption occasions and depth of consumption on each occasion with the same consumer. Both lead to increase in revenue but they impact consumers differently.

Now, India is a country with low penetration for most categories. As per the IRS (Indian Readership Survey which measures readership and consumption of various fast moving consumer goods [FMCG] throughout the country), you would notice that most categories have low penetration in India. And this is as true of urban India as it is of rural India, meaning that access is not the issue. Now, unless you have come very late into the category and are content to take market share from other players, chances are you should be leading growth with penetration. The mega brands of Indian FMCG have been built on the basis of aggressive penetration strategy built on good value for money, mass distribution, production and communication strategy. So generally speaking, you are well advised to keep penetration as the centrepiece of your brand strategy in most categories.

For the purpose of getting more bang out of the buck, brand managers can do market prioritization of various segments of their markets to decide the level of input intensity in each market. This would be based on ranking the ones with maximum returns as top priority and lesser ones after them, through a priority 1, priority 2, priority 3 kind of approach.

Below is a suggested prioritization grid that we followed for Lay's potato chips in the launch years.

Figure 6.6: Prioritization matrix

Segment	Priority 1	Priority 2	Priority 3
Geographical	North, West	South	East
Demographic (SEC/age)	SEC A, B, 8–15	SEC A, 8–25	SEC A, 8–25
Psychographic	Experimentative, outgoing	Variety-seeking	Taste fanatics
Behavioural	Outdoors	Value-seeking	Economy

As the figure shows, while the brand's overall segment was the country, led by kids and tweens who enjoyed taste and fun with chips, we then cut this national approach with regional segmentation to maximize the impact.

Accordingly, 60 per cent revenue was expected to come from the North and West because in these areas, the category of chips, through products of small-scale players, was already developed. However, to get early adoption, we decided to chase upper class kids and teens with an appetite for trying new tastes, especially when they were outdoors. Communication and media was cut in keeping with that strategy to maximize trials and repeats. For South, we chased a wider target audience from a media perspective, and launched more flavours (especially Tomato) for the variety-seeking consumers in large packs, hoping to draw from the behaviour of their banana chips consumption.

For the taste fanatics of East who liked flavours like 'Papdi Chaat' of Uncle Chips, Masala was placed in higher numbers in the ubiquitous Lay's racks, and regional creatives were made showcasing a low entry price of Rs 5 for the value-conscious consumer who was on the go, near cinema theatres and 'paras' during puja festival, making maximum impact.

From a timing perspective, Priority 2 and Priority 3 (P2 and P3) markets were launched after getting initial traction in North. Before that, the whole model was piloted in Delhi and Punjab to optimize flavours and media and distribution strategy before going national. This strategy of sequential targeting helped reduce expenses and maximize success.

Taking stock of this phased strategy after three years, we found that penetration of the category of chips had increased by nearly 300 basis points for Lay's chips due to this intense targeted approach. However, as the markets started to mature in North and West, the imminent question was how to increase frequency of consumption amongst those who had tried chips in the first few years.

Segmentation studies in Delhi and Punjab revealed that consumers loved the crispiness and quality of chips (bite, saltiness, limited oil pick-up) but reported fatigue with the taste of salt and masala. While they were inclined to try chips on many more occasions (tested through some leading questions in research), they were currently only having it outside the home.

From this study, three flavours were tested that would give incremental sales, meaning they would be consumed in addition to and not in lieu of the current bag of salt and masala. These were American Style Cream and Onion, Spanish Tomato Tango and Italian Style Cheesy Paprika. These flavours were launched over a year, after intense testing to increase the frequency of consumption and not cannibalize the previous flavours. After undertaking an elaborate research technique called TURF (Total Unduplicated Reach and Frequency), which tested how much more incremental consumption would ensue from the flavour, these flavours were chosen and launched.

Alongside, new television creatives were made that cued new consumption occasions for the youth. In college cafeterias, while watching television or just hanging out at their favourite places. After nearly a year, when only two flavours survived, the consumption occasions had widened and frequency of consumption amongst core users had gone up from four bags in a year to almost five. Simultaneously, higher grammage bags were increased so more chips were consumed for every bag opened on occasions when collective consumption was prevalent.

While this was on, markets in East and South were still chasing penetration strategy, getting fresh users through distribution and aggressive pricing. Tomato flavour which flopped in North, did surprisingly well in West and South. We realized that no single solution would work for the whole country and we would have to segment the market as per regional preference for taste and development of the category.

Frequency of consumption can be led by most brands through different variants that offer multiple taste experiences; or through building different points of consumption through communication and special packs like the large party packs of Lay's and Pepsi; or through repeated reminders of consumption, especially for impulse categories (unlike planned grocery items that are part of household monthly ration purchase) to nudge consumers towards consumption often and at varied points.

Hence, penetration and frequency can be pursued for the same brand at the same time. However, in reality, most marketers have pursued penetration strategy for the following reasons.

- India being a country with low disposable income, there is always an opportunity to scrape the bottom of the barrel no matter how low you go down the income pyramid. The shampoo category, which was thought to be an urban phenomenon, exploded in upcountry markets by the launch of shampoo sachets which found usage in daily wage earners because of low single cash pay-out and the sheer improvement in the quality of cleaning experience. Thus, most categories, either through downsizing or reformulating recipes, will still gain more and more consumers no matter how long they have been around.

- Most brands will have a set of loyal consumers but also some fence-sitters and some new entrants. This is inevitable given the fragmented nature of retail and dispersion of consumers across a wide country where consumers can't always access their brands. Also, some consumers show a high propensity to keep flirting in and out of the category. These fence-sitters and the indifferent consumers who walk in and out of the category based on availability with no view of brands form the long tail of a brand's consumption profile.

- For any brand, about 30–35 per cent consumers could lie in this segment. If a brand chases frequency of consumption alone (ignoring mass production, distribution and extensive communication that penetration strategy entails), then the long tail of consumption can be impacted adversely, which cannot be met by increased consumption of loyal consumers. For this reason, an ongoing penetration strategy makes a lot of sense for brands with a large turnover that wish to sustain high growth levels.

- Most large companies depend on scale to keep input costs low and maximize returns on invested capital. Penetration strategy that targets a large number of consumers ensures that all fixed and variable costs are well utilized with reducing input cost per unit as business expands, improving the P&L.

- Also, penetration strategy always augurs well for the future. In a country where income is rising and urbanization is an irreversible reality, catching consumers young invariably helps in building the foundation for strong future consumption. By just chasing high frequency strategy, we could severely cripple future growth opportunities for a growing country like India.

Segmentation and targeting are therefore absolutely critical to marry your two goals in marketing: finding your consumer and knowing him/her and then finding the most cost-effective way to reach them.

So, now that we have understood the consumer a little better, it's time to dive into her mind, where the battle for image, preference and share of the brand is being fought feverishly day after day.

Week 10

How Do I Position My Brand?

Having understood Segmentation and Targeting in the previous week, it's time in Week 10 to brush up on the soft qualities of office art that will go a long way in helping you build and sustain success in the office environment. Managing the power equations in office becomes critical when you are leading big projects with high impact and several stakeholders. Therefore, it's important to build a solid alignment as you start to build your brand and career.

Office art: Striking effective cross-alliances

The first step towards forging effective cross-alliances in the company is to figure out who are the real influencers. A word of caution here: the idea is not to get political and pander to those in power but to rally all the resources behind one's project. It's important to acquire this ability but it's equally important to direct it rightly to avoid becoming a victim to its negative side effects.

So, if your project is based on deep consumer insight, make sure the insight manager is your supporter; in fact, make him your spokesperson. Alternatively, if procurement is at the heart of your new idea—when, for example, you are launching the nation's first organic products or a breakthrough washing machine based on the purchase of some critical equipment from an OEM (original equipment manufacturer)—make sure the head of procurement owns your project like it is his own baby as you accord him due respect and importance. Influence should be brought to bear based on the nature of the project.

However, influencers who wield power may not always be the functional leaders. There are informal channels of power ruled by people on account of their expertise on a subject, or being in a pivotal position of flow of information, or having access to resources, or through knowing other people or through knowing the top man who calls the shots. Identify who exercises disproportionate influence because of their informal authority and win their approval.

In your search for influencers, you will hit people who are approvers, opponents, fence-sitters and passive rivals. Opponents and passive rivals are dangerous whether they are overtly visible or not. You need to understand their reason for being a counterweight against you and carefully tackle it. They may oppose you because they are comfortable with the status quo, or they may be threatened by an emerging situation which they fear will undermine their power, or they simply envy your rapid march upwards. You will have to approach them carefully to assure them, assuage their fear or maybe outright dismiss their disparaging moves with your firmness. The fence-sitters, on the other hand, are a piquant lot and you may have to figure out what drives their indecisiveness. Are they just undecided or are they indifferent or are they waiting to ascertain which way the wind is blowing to take sides later? Finally, the approvers have to be turned into evangelists for your cause by recognizing them and giving them power.

As you go around winning people, make sure you put a good mix of logos or logic, pathos or emotional reasons, and ethos or appeal to higher values. Different people have different keys and you have to develop your senses to know how to unlock them to support you.

Once you have laid out your social map in office, visit it often and constantly recharge it with newer reasons so, when the time comes, you can put it to good use. If you don't, you will end up appearing selfish to others, only visiting them when you need them. Care should also be taken to keep matters at a healthy professional level, avoiding excessive personal conversation to avoid undermining the professional efficacy of these cross-alliances.

Now that we have some sense of how the minds of people work in office, it's time to turn to building our brand competencies to understand how the mind of the consumer works at the most subtle level.

Positioning: winning in the consumer's mind

This is where the best of marketers will take birth and bloom, and if they fail to understand the intricacy of this art, they will be consigned to mediocrity.

Positioning comes into play between the want and demand of a brand. It overcomes barriers and promises benefits so that in the consumer's mind, where the theatre of ideas plays out, your brand emerges a winner, prevailing over all other competitive brands. It defines the expectation of the experience of the brand and after consumption, validates or repudiates it to make a total brand impression.

It's also the word that is most abused in marketing jargon, standing frivolously as a substitute for location, perspective or reason to exist. It's therefore worth our time to undertake an academic drill to unravel positioning to unleash its full impact.

Positioning: what it means

Rosser Reeves calls positioning the art of selecting, out of a number of unique selling propositions, the one that will get maximum sales.

Philip Kotler (*Marketing Essentials*, Prentice-Hall, 1984) calls it 'arranging for a product to occupy a clear, distinctive and desirable place in the market and the minds of the target consumers'. Beckman, Kurtz, Boone (*Foundations of Marketing*, Holt Rinehart & Winston, 1986) refers to the consumer's perception of the product's attributes, use, quality, advantages and disadvantages in relation to competing brands. Raymond D. Hehman (*Product Management*, Dow Jones-Irwin, 1984) simplifies it to suggest, 'Positioning is your product as the consumer thinks of it. Since the consumer is ultimate user of the product, the consumer's perception of your product is what your product really is.' F. Beaven Ennis (*Handbook of Modern Marketing*, Victor P. Buell (ed.), McGraw-Hill, 1986) points out that it's about the 'identification of the exclusive niche in the market or the creation of a unique perception of the product that satisfies an unfulfilled consumer and serves to distinguish it from competing alternatives'.

Phew, if you feel academically brow-beaten, here is the simplified gist you need to bear in mind.

> Positioning is the perception of the brand in the consumer's mind and heart that connects his/her need with the brand's unique benefits over and above competitive claims.

Because it's a complex set of images and impressions, it comprises functional attributes, emotional pay-offs and associations that can't always be rationally coded but can be built over time to create a niche for the brand that stands out. If this summation encapsulates all that it is, it poses the next questions: how does positioning form in the brain and how can it be managed to the brand manager's advantage? For that, we will have to step out of marketing into the domain of psychology to understand 'memory structures' before we delve into how to capitalize on it. It's important to grasp this to acquire the faith in positioning so it becomes the holy grail of everything we do in marketing.

Positioning: the real psychology underneath

Before we understand positioning, stepping back to understand the human world of knowledge and learning would be beneficial, to gain a holistic perspective. Since our world is replete with infinite things, people, relationships, and our ability to take cognisance of them is limited, we structure it up with words, concepts and images that help us navigate a varied world for meeting our specific needs.

Further, in the interest of efficiency, we form judgements and opinions and cling to them steadfastly, repudiating or validating them only occasionally. This has become our evolutionary advantage, also allowing us to amass a huge amount of information and knowledge.

Why are we going so far back in our lives to understand brands? Well, because our brands are no differently handled when they enter the human world. Just as we assimilate the unknown world by creating new words, concepts and impressions, so also we process brands through words, concepts and images. For brands to be understood in the way we want to, it's important that we message them sharply, accurately and consistently so that we create a desirable memory structure that would dispose consumers positively towards our brand.

If we look closely at how the human mind works, a few relevant details come to our attention that can be productively employed for building brand equity. Memory gets built primarily through three routes:

- Semantic memory: built through words and associated descriptions. Such as the sun is bright and also feels hot when you are exposed to it for a long time.
- Episodic memory: based on specific events like having Maggi during your hostel days, or relishing KitKat during exam breaks.
- Procedural memory: is non-declarative or unconscious. Unlike the other two which are conscious, this one gets built without

one's recall. For instance, riding a cycle or swimming. However, once ingrained, it becomes a part of involuntary action. When brands become everyday usually as a result of loyalty, then they almost slip into procedural memory from where they cannot be shaken out easily. Like choosing Amul Butter or brushing with Colgate every morning—you have done it so many times that you can't recall anything about it. You turn to these brands almost reflexively.

Thus, to build our brand memory structure, we need to have several stimuli: semantic, episodic, maybe even procedural. Eventually, the more pathways you create in the brain of the consumer, the better the recall, based on the adage that 'neurons that fire together, wire together'. It becomes essential that to develop a brand, we must build a host of associations around the brand so that consumers get intersected with multiple reminders of the brand, thereby strengthening the original memory and driving loyalty.

Why are we saying all this? Because, to build brands, you need to have a central idea which is unwaveringly consistent and also has many manifestations. One that improves both the extent and the quality of brand recall. Thus, you don't remember just how well Dettol saves you from infection, but you also think of its myriad applications: during sickness in hospital, or to prevent sickness at home in the everyday mopping.

Positioning is that critical umbilical cord between the consumer and the brand through which consistent perceptions about the brand are relayed. Given all that we have discussed before, brands have to make a crisp impression and do it consistently. In reality, however, the communication is not single-minded and seldom consistent. Due to this, many brands are lost in a clutter of their own making.

So how does one make a solid memory structure of the brand in the consumer's mind as there is so little space for brands, and even fewer opportunities for brands to communicate in this noisy environment?

For starters, we have to write the positioning statement of the brand with great rigour and discipline. It's surprising that many big brands don't have one consistent statement that endures for many years, and many small brands haven't even got around to doing that.

This is easier expressed than executed. So, before we deep-dive into this process, let's understand the kinds of positioning options available in the market to avoid the common pitfalls in this area.

Kinds of positioning

What are some stellar examples of positioning? A few brands stand out as excellent examples of well-defined positioning statements that have created value for the consumers and the company. Since positioning statements are companies' internal secret, it's often not that easy to get them. But brand taglines offer a good peek into the brand's positioning platforms. Below are a few instructive examples.

- 7Up: 'The Uncola'. It puts the drink in a class apart from the Pepsis and Cokes, the leaders in the market, setting up a viable alternative for consumers.
- Duracell: 'No battery lasts longer'. It takes the primary concern of batteries—shelf life and makes a tall claim with the alkaline batteries that indeed outperform competing options.
- Nike: 'Just do it.' Based on the truthful human insight that if we stopped worrying and started acting, we would achieve more.
- KFC: 'Finger lickin' good.' If we really love the food, then we invariably lick our fingers after we've eaten to prolong the experience that we don't want to end.
- Apple's Mac: "Everything is easier on a Mac." A clear allusion to IBM's forbidding machines which consumers could get relief from.

- Federal Express: 'When it absolutely, positively has to be there overnight.' Harping on the primary need for a courier, speed, it emphasizes the keyword 'overnight' to anchor the superlative benefit.
- Subway: 'Eat fresh.' A counter to the junk-ridden fast food options through its healthy alternative of fresh ingredients.
- Adidas: 'Impossible is nothing.' Exhorting people to tap their unknown potential through a time-tested adage that sits well with sports gear designed for high performance.
- Burger King: 'Have it your way.' Menu flexibility combined with a standard taste, every time.

From the above examples, we get a broad understanding of the grounds on which we can position our brands. Thus, we could build the basis of positioning through a) product attribute (Duracell, KFC), b) competition (7Up, Subway), c) consumer experience (Apple), or d) perspective rooted in human insight (Nike, Adidas).

Closer home in India, we found that positioning can be approached from the following standpoints:

Company positioning: A host of Indian brands draw their might and relevance because of their age-old company legacy. Tata, ITC, Godrej—these groups have launched innumerable brands purely on consumers' assumed response that if they are established in some other category, however unrelated, they must be good. So your car, watch, salt, house, financial services, IT consulting, steel, coffee, all can come from one group called Tata.

Legacy positioning: A host of small local players grown on the tutelage of their patriarchs take this brand positioning. They are prevalent across lower social classes and town classes having come up from the ranks. Brands of masalas (like MDH), tobacco, real estate and pickles draw their strong legitimacy from having been around for a long time.

Umbrella positioning: This kind of positioning establishes a name as being expert in one area and then allows all related ancillary categories and sub-categories of a kind to spawn underneath. Maruti built its brand on the promise of reliability, economy, widespread availability and service and then went on to dominate segments from economy to luxury across various passenger car segments.

Colgate is another classic example of umbrella positioning. All Colgate products, saving the differentiation of ingredients (Blue Gel, Active Salt, Total), highlight the Colgate positioning of dental care from the dentist's hands consistently.

Ingredient positioning: This draws strength from the power of ingredients such as Dabur, which extols Ayurvedic medicine through a range of its product or Vicco Laboratories' cream based on the highly believable goodness of turmeric. Many companies have taken this route, especially if they have grown on the back of a strong line of products where the unique selling proposition is the raw material.

Benefit Positioning: Dettol, Harpic and Lysol have taken first aid, disinfection and hygiene as the primary benefit for consumers, winning many loyalists. Pidilite Industries has exaggerated the simple benefit of sticking for its brand Fevicol so convincingly that the word 'Fevi' can be prefixed anywhere and the benefit proposition sticks: Fevikwik, Fevistick, Fevicryl.

Fun positioning: Impulse brands, especially in the space of confectionary, take this route with thumping success. Perfetti with its many brands has delighted consumers with the proposition as much as the product. Alpenliebe's unabashed indulgence is expressed through 'laalach aha lap lap'. Mentos, a fresh mint flavour for perky youngsters, sets the brain thinking or 'Dimag ki batti jala de' with some iconic creatives. Such creatives have little to do with functional appeal, but their humour tickles the consumer's funny bone and ensures the remembrance of brands.

Feature positioning: This approach is seen in the mobile phone landscape which is dotted with feature after feature based on camera power. Oppo's F3 series gives dual-selfies, Vivo's 24 MP gives clearer shots: 'A picture defines a moment—Clear Shot, Clear Moment', Micromax has Canvas Infinity, full vision display with 18:9. In fact, even iPhone focuses on the unbelievable photo-experience of its consumers. However, when everyone converges on the same experience, positioning gets compromised to mere numeric comparison of screen-size and mega-pixels.

Competitive positioning: Referenced to competition or the prevailing trend in the category, this perspective gives the brand a head start if it is well articulated. Pepsi was launched as the choice of a new generation, targeting the classic and somewhat old world of Coke. Avis, the car rental agency, made a virtue of being number 2 but elevated its secondary status by saying 'We try harder.'

Emotional positioning: Here, the fulfilment of the user's emotional need is captured. 'The complete man' of Raymond or 'The best a man can get' of Gillette indicates the emotional pay-off that the consumer of the brand can expect. Such positioning approaches can get vague over time if sufficient functional aspects are not regularly infused in the brand.

The above examples are not an exhaustive list of positioning options but they indicate the range of possibilities open to us. Now that we have spanned the menu of positioning, let's evaluate how to write a precise positioning statement.

Writing a positioning statement

A good positioning statement covers the vital aspects of the offer and leaves out what is superfluous. A positioning statement must cover the following:

- Whom is the product for?
- What is the consumer need the brand is resolving?
- What is the brand name?
- Which category is being spoken of?
- What is the functional benefit—the key benefit that satisfies the need and is the reason to believe (or RTB) the brand promise?
- Who are the other players in the category? Companies have to take stock of what is in the market and not be in denial, to avoid being a me-too and to stand out in the marketplace.
- What is the emotional benefit for the consumer should he embrace the brand?

Let's write a few positioning statements to get a handle on this art, which is often overlooked or avoided or confused with related things like brand concept or advertising tagline. Though, in essence, it is at the heart of everything a brand does and it also inspires future possibilities.

Following the above template and going back to Britannia Industries, which has segmented and positioned its products in the large biscuit category successfully, we get some instructive examples. Tiger biscuits (product and category) are for those moms who want their kids (for whom) 'roaring' with energy (emotional and functional benefit) because it has vitamins, iron and calcium up to the extent of 25 per cent of their daily need (RTB). The benefit, brand and RTB are compactly held together by a unifying 'position' that also sets it apart from the generic glucose biscuit brand that sells on the street.

Likewise, Marie Gold (not just Marie, to differentiate on a basic category name with a suffix) is for women who seek to accomplish more every day, partnering the lonely tea-moment while being low in fat and cholesterol. A variant, Vita Marie, comes with the extra nutrition of vitamins.

NutriChoice is positioned as power packed snacks (creating a new category of healthy snacking) for people who chase a healthy way of life (emotional benefit) with the benefit of oats and easy digestibility.

The indulgence segment has been tapped with cream treats, Jim Jam (at entry level) and Bourbon (for showing off your wickedly smooth side, 'the chocolate lover's favourite guilt trip'). Pure Magic ('chocolate artistry' for the cognoscenti) is positioned for wanton indulgence, overriding the demographic straight lines.

Little Hearts, lightly flirting between snack and biscuit categories, are 'light crunchy melt-in-your-mouth biscuits for chatting up with friends'. A clean and distinctive positioning complementing the product experience, incontrovertibly.

Positioning is relatively easier if the company operates in different product categories within one industry. Dabur has carried the brand assurance across different categories, while staying anchored in the goodness of Ayurveda. Dabur Honey is positioned for 30-plus girls, with the goodness of honey for skin and digestion. Dabur Chyawanprash, which is the crowning glory at the top of the portfolio, is positioned on general immunity on the RTB of a science and 2500-year-old recipe based on amla (Indian gooseberry) and herbs.

Kinds of mind maps: Cluster, Perceptual, Multidimensional

Reading the above, one can clearly infer the need for knowing what the critical determinants of a category are, which lead consumers to choose one brand over another; and the relative importance of these. A study of these attributes or variables is absolutely critical to understand the strength of the positioning of one's brand. From this, one can make corrections or enforce what's working well for one's brand.

So, how do you know what's working for the consumer? Without getting into the full academic depth of the following approaches, a comparative overview is being taken here to help determine the right technique for one's brand.

Spoken generally, you may want to know:

- Where your brand is in the consumer's mind with respect to other brands on a set of attributes. This is called image profiling.
- What variables drive consumers' preference in choosing brands? This is captured in factor analysis.
- How do various brands in the category cluster in consumers' perceptions with respect to your brand? This is understood by cluster analysis.
- How do various brands (within a category or even with respect to proximal categories) interact with each other? This can be diagnosed by multidimensional scaling.
- How does my brand stand versus other brands in a single visual appreciation? This can be inferred by perceptual mapping using some of the techniques mentioned above.
- Finally, what is the preferred positioning for my brand through preference mapping and even for designing new products through conjoint analysis.

Now, you may have access to this data if your brand is well researched. The details below will help you connect the data for making better choices for your brand. But if it is missing, which is likely, then you can do some estimations, or some quick dipstick researches since these are required for making better, informed choices.

Let's understand these with some examples.

Image profiling: If you want to know the relative position of your brand vis-à-vis other competitive brands on a set of related variables, image profiling tells you exactly that, variable by variable. For instance, if you want to profile your brand of detergent versus four others on variables like cleaning ability, protection of colour, easy solubility, value for money and gentleness, then you make consumers give each brand a score on a scale of 0 to 5 and this is how the result would look like for your analysis:

Figure 7.1: Image profiling analysis

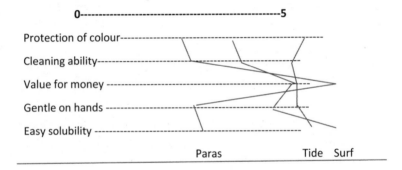

All figures in the above chart are for illustration purposes only.

Indicative data for explanation

As a brand manager of Surf, you can be happy that you outscore your local rival, Paras, on most attributes except value for money (this high score would indicate that consumers really think low price is value for money even though their experience on other variables is not good—this befuddling reality often confronts managers), but Tide has an advantage with respect to easy solubility and is also not far behind on value for money. This analysis reveals the opportunity for brands to improve or, if the situation cannot be redeemed, then be cognizant of what one is strong in and play to one's strength. This is also a perfectly good strategy since one cannot score high on all variables. Here, there is a clear opportunity for Surf to redefine value for money, also based on high performance on all variables, and make consumers consider and change their view in favour of the brand.

Factor Analysis: From the above emerges the question: How can you know which attributes matter to consumers, so you are sure that you are focused on what truly matters to them? Factor analysis allows marketers to look at a host of variables (you start by making a laundry list) and reduce them to a few on which brands can be assessed relative to each other. A mathematical technique is used in finding the correlation between different variables to arrive at the latent variable underneath these that is impacting them together. At the end, you can reduce several variables down to two variables that account for maximum variance by aggregating the variables along two factors, and then you proceed to plot your brand and the competitors on a two-dimensional map. This technique allows you to evaluate your nearness to the variable that matters compared to competition. The example below will help, if you are still foggy.

If you are evaluating coffee, you are dealing with variables like: most popular brand (1) or least popular brand (2), for contemporary (3) or traditional people (4), for lower (5) or upper class people (6), with a strong bitter coffee taste (7) or a weak one (8), for old (9) or young people (10) and then run the factor analysis, getting two primary axes as below. After that, brands A, B and C are plotted with respect to these two variables to obtain the factor analysis map as below:

Figure 7.2: Factor analysis map

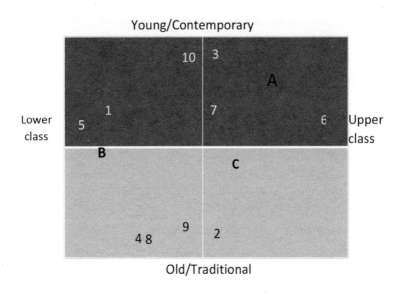

All figures in the above chart are for illustration purposes only.

From the above, one can infer that brand A is clearly youthful, with the times for the upper class lying in the top quadrant whereas brand C is old and traditional for the middle class. In this case, if you are the brand manager of C and your brand equity revolves around heritage for the middle class, you are all right. If not and you want to be for the youth, then you clearly have a lot of catching up to do. Thus, factor analysis helps managers see their brand with respect to the factors that have maximum impact on the category (or account for maximum variance between variables) and evaluate where they stand vis-à-vis their strategy.

Cluster analysis: If there are many categories and you wish to know how they can be bunched in groups to set them apart and find the relative position of your brand versus others, cluster analysis comes in handy. Through a set of questions that are meant to pull similar and dissimilar brands together, brands fall into a pattern as per consumers' appreciation of them. For instance, if you ask consumers how they see biscuits, chips, noodles, MFD, samosa, chola batura, upma, dosa on a continuum of health and taste, you get them bunched as below and the distance between them (correlated with the score they get on various attribute questions) indicates which categories are seen close to each other and which are distant.

Figure 7.3: Cluster analysis map

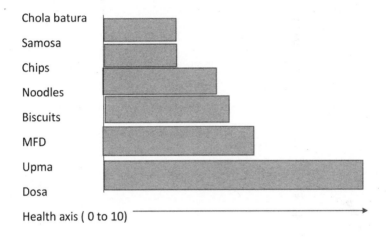

All figures in the above chart are for illustration purposes only.

The cluster analysis reveals the ascending order of those categories associated with health with 0 being the lowest in health and 10 the highest. Chola batura and samosa make one cluster, then come chips and noodles followed by biscuits and MFD which have similar scores, with home-made options featuring the highest in health. The health continuum below indicates the distance between these clusters. Knowing this, one can understand the limits and opportunities of the category one's brand plays in, and accordingly position the brand to take business from other categories. Thus, a chip can take the market of noodles outside its category, but may struggle to get into the market of a snack like upma given the large distance in consumer association of these categories with health.

Also, if one wants to position one's brand differently from the category it belongs to, then it must take codes of another category and consciously plant that in the consumer's consideration to get the required benefit. Thus, baked chips can claim to be as healthy as a dosa or upma, targeting consumption occasions of the home-made snacks.

Multidimensional scaling: This technique goes one step further to estimate on different dimensions involved in the consumer perception of the product (such as taste, texture, thickness, sourness, sweetness, ease of spread for a category like tomato ketchup) and how brands like Maggi, Kissan, Heinz and Cremica are placed with respect to each other. The result could be then put in a scale as below:

Figure 7.4 Preference table

Preferred from/to	Maggi	Kissan	Heinz	Cremica
Maggi	0	30	15	10
Kissan	40	0	15	30
Heinz	30	10	0	20
Cremica	60	30	20	0

All figures in the above chart are for illustration purposes only.

Thus, Maggi consumers can shift to Kissan in 30 per cent cases, but only 15 and 10 per cent to Heinz and Cremica, whereas Cremica consumers can switch to Maggi in large numbers. This shows the likelihood of switching to other brands especially in favour of market leader Maggi; whereas the switching is a lot less likely to happen in favour of other brands when Maggi is not available.

The data from the above can be plotted on a perceptual map based on the two critical axes (done from a technique similar to factor analysis) of taste (distinct and regular) and price (economy to premium) to determine the position of the brands with respect to each other. This is very useful for brand managers to get a relative spatial sense of their brands on relevant axes.

Figure 7.5: Perceptual map

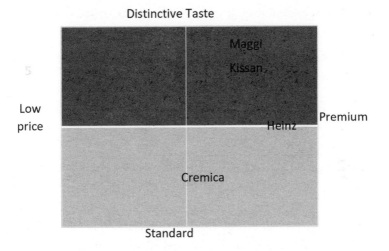

Finally, preference mapping and conjoint analysis, without labouring their techniques, offer solutions if you have a dilemma between two or three close variables for pivoting your positioning. It includes looking at the variables with respect to the impact they make on the consumer decision matrix and helps select the ones that are more material to long-term adoption of the brand. In cases where the current brand is not modifiable to reflect emerging needs with its positioning boundaries, it even helps in launching new, innovative products that can be positioned afresh.

Now, all this seems like a tremendous academic load this far. If you have these researches, you are fortunate in having the opportunity to connect the data to understand what variables matter (factor analysis), how your brand stands versus others many variables (image profiling), and how it bunches with respect to other brands (cluster). This will enable you to make right choices for the brand based on preference patterns (multidimensional scaling) and perceptual maps.

If you don't have access to the data, then you must run through these steps and, with a mix of dipsticks, other primary or secondary research and discussion with the research team, try to contextualize your brand correctly. A perspective born out of these analyses is priceless in guiding positioning discussions.

Positioning must-dos

Upon scanning the market, we arrived at the following watch-outs for positioning:

Grab No. 1: There is a big premium on being number one in a category. Consumers eventually equate the category with you and are willing to give you the benefit of attributing most advantages of that category to you. For instance, copiers are Xerox, Chyawanprash is Dabur, a shaving system is Gillette and so on. Why this happens is a matter of debate, but one who raises his hand first becomes the upholder of the benefits in that category. It's very difficult to uproot the first one because, once consumers have granted one brand the status of being the first, they cannot be made to re-evaluate easily. So, if there is a category where you are the first one or have a dominant share, make sure you claim that status. It works just as we remember the first person to walk on the moon, the first to climb Everest, but never the second one. Just as it works in real life, so it works with brands also.

The downside of becoming number one is that you could become synonymous with the category and get taken for granted; for example, when people ask for a Xerox, meaning a copy, but are using an HP machine. Yes, that happens, but not after you have grabbed a large market share and it's a better problem to have than living in the shadow of market leader.

Redefine the category or create one: Since you can't always choose the time you step into a category, you can't always get the benefit of being the first one. But you have the option of creating the reference framework for being the first one. In other words, cause consumers to look at a pre-existing category in a new way or create a whole new segment and urge your user to look at it as though he was looking at it for the first time. This way, you will become number one.

So, you can create a shampoo plus conditioner, or a family sports utility vehicle, or an air-conditioner with an in-built inverter and make your playing arena so unique that you become the number one. Redefining an old category is the only way to become no. 1 in spite of coming in late. If done well and convincingly, this can be as good as entering a new category in the consumer's eye.

Truth is perception, create truth through perception: As human beings, we seek and treasure truth as it becomes the guiding principle of life. But truth is a result of perception formed, accidentally or meditatively, by the human mind. What if that could be managed? Well, brands do just that.

By choosing to cast themselves in a certain light and doing so repeatedly and honestly, brands can create an unassailable impression which becomes the truth of the category they rule. Consumers will love and trust this, turning into fierce loyalists of your brand.

But to turn a perception into a brand truth, you have to work hard. You have to choose what matters to the consumer through right insight and positioning and then establish it with tenacity.

A whimper does not work in setting a new idea into the consumer's mind; you have to scream and be noticed over all others. Pepsi broke into the saturated world of Coke consumers and set up a whole new narrative as the choice of new generation—but with marketing decibels of millions. That is the only way perceptions can be formed to take on an earlier truth of Coke being the classic do-all beverage.

Perception matters as much as the product, drive it: A lot of work goes into creating the perfect product on the assumption that if it performs well, it will succeed. But before the product is tried and even after its services have been consumed, there sits the perception. If that isn't favourable, the brand promise has a poor or no start and even subsequently, it may not be realized or appreciated.

Perception can make an engineering wonder like Nano fail or a host of me-too ideas, as in the space of real estate or cell phones, click because of sheer perception management. Casting the web of expectations far and well and triggering and reflecting the consumer's positive response is as critical as the product's performance. In the ultimate analysis, marketing is a battle of perception much more than competition between products with distinctive features. This is especially true in the digital world where consumer reviews and opinions have become very significant in driving purchase for other consumers.

Let positioning drive projection of self on the brand: The world acquires its character by superimposition of our self-projection on it. There is no reality independent of our construction of it. Brands, much like everything else we perceive in life, can be made to project the personality of the user and thereby endear itself to them. Positioning by honestly reflecting the consumer and resonating with her by being empathetic can become the mirror of the consumer. If that happens, brands have hit home. Without it, they are just a distant commodity. Think of brands like Apple, Nike and Fabindia, and you can appreciate how they have become the extended representation of the consumer who patronizes them.

Own a singular idea; if possible, even a singular word: The market is cluttered, consumers have no time to spare. Only one idea per brand will go down, only one or two words about a brand can be remembered. Everything over this is wasteful, in fact, damaging to brand recall as it creates confounding noise that drowns out whatever little brand message could have been considered by the consumer. Thus, FedEx is 'overnight' delivery, Domino's appeals when 'Hungry kya?', Fevicol 'sticks' anything, Volvo is 'safety', Mercedes is 'engineering' and Duracell is 'long lasting'.

Staying focused, dropping all that is redundant in terms of sound and image, is the surest way to grab eyeballs. Even better, it's the best way to make consumers ask for you even before you show up. But for that, you need to choose what matters, very carefully, and ruthlessly ignore or reject any other opportunity to say or do more.

How do you own a singular idea? Make sure nobody else is using it, since two companies cannot chase the same idea or word. Make doubly sure that you own the primary benefit of that category, meaning it should be the most material to the need-fulfilment of that category or segment of the category that has been chosen, such as safety for Volvo, or milk nourishment for Amul. Lastly, converge all brand expressions to the one idea or word, at every opportunity.

Be in the first two or three, if you can't be no. 1, with a narrow gap: Consumers are willing to give only two or three brands a chance in a defined category and that too if they are close by, not distant in their consideration. Then, switching can happen but beyond that, it is usually not possible. If you are not fitting in the first two or three, either abandon or recast the benefits of a category to define a new playground. Beverages had Pepsi and Coke, and Sprite could enter only by creating a new clear lemon segment. In toothpaste,

Colgate has a formidable majority with only Pepsodent as a second rival, until Sensodyne came and carved a niche as a solution for sensitive gums.

If we forcibly fit brands into a category that seems too distant to consumers, they just won't stick in the assessment of that category by the consumer. For instance, mouthwash cannot take the same regularity and compulsiveness of a toothpaste even if marketers try, because it's just too far apart. Or a digital watch from Apple will not be considered in the same way as an iconic style brand like Rolex. Categories have borders and unless they are opened with strong reason and emotion, they should be respected to avoid going counter-intuitive to consumers' perception.

In conclusion, assess if you are within two or three brands in the brain-shelf of that category; there is no point trying to jostle another one. Create a new shelf or walk away from an almirah that is taken.

Follower brands can position themselves counter to leaders unabashedly: Every category will have a counter view. If propounded well, it can create space even in a monopolistic domain and make consumer sense as they get it immediately, thereby making positioning easy. As Avis countered Hertz, acknowledging its number two status and valorizing it by making it a reason to work harder. As Titan took on the goliath HMT to make it history by launching a quartz watch and styling it as a counter to the values of durability and lineage of HMT. Or Savlon took the bite of Dettol and made it a viable alternative (though Dettol hit back equating bite with efficacy, with some success).

In fact, strong counter ideas can make the original leaders appear like followers, even making them bite the dust, if positioning is consistently and cogently marketed. You can become the newer version, positioning the old as fuddy-duddy, reflecting consumers' emerging aspirations.

One brand, one idea: For the most part, a brand can only stand for one benefit, that too of a category. Coke could not make a success of the clothes line it launched adventurously; Horlicks and Cadbury biscuits made no impact when they brought the strength of their HFD category into a seemingly related space of nutrition.

Consumers' attention can be grabbed once and can be grabbed for one reason only. Trying to make it work too hard in another space for another reason will just not stick because the justification of two categories is different and consumers rarely pass the equity earned in one category to another. Only in related categories like Amul's dairy products or Maruti's economy to mainstream segment can the brand be stretched (think of Amul in snacks, or Maruti in bikes and the oddness becomes apparent) but otherwise, consumers are averse to having their affection taken for granted across two categories.

Positioning over promotion, always: Promotions scream 'Buy now, better now than later'. They exercise urgency and economy but not the essentials of a brand. Positioning justifies the why of the brand constantly, which goes deeper in the consumer psyche and stretches further in time. Positioning and promotion work counter to each other. One is a short-term kick, the other is long-term health. You cannot replace one with the other any more than you can make alcohol work for both happiness and vitality.

Hence, choose one over the other, never erring to think one can substitute the other. And if possible, position more often than promote. In fact, strong positioning can preclude tactical promotion for a long time.

Reject some, gain a lot more: Positioning is fundamentally about making choices. You have to let go of calling out some benefits, some features, just because you have them in the product, and emphasize only and only the exceptional. Vicks could have been a general balm for many pains but it chose to focus only on colds and then went on to maximize every opportunity in that segment (to build a formidable market even in a niche space compared to prevailing balms like Amrutanjan and Iodex) like rubbing it on the chest and back, and even below a congested nose as an inhalation.

In positioning, the winning trick is drilling deeper in the same well rather than drilling wells all across. That may mean more pain now, since gains are faster when you cover the market horizontally, tapping every available opportunity. But it also runs out faster, apart from making your brand vulnerable to attacks from many more competitors. Doing everything is like some retail brands that offer everything, specialize in nothing and eventually get down to discounts to attract consumers. Doing a select few things makes a swashbuckling hit brand like Marlboro, which sells at a premium and commands loyalty among many who value its cowboy's image due to its relevant imagery (even when paradoxically, there are hardly any cowboys around).

Bad honest is better than good dishonest: Positioning respects honesty because, in a sincere conversation with the consumer, transparency pays. If your product has a perceived negative, then transparently communicate the reason and win consumers' consent. Dettol stings but it works harder on the germs so you are safe. Your deodorant kills 80 per cent germs against the imagined 100 per cent of competition and for consumers, it could be more believable than hyper-claims. Candour can disarm consumers, winning their unqualified approval whereas excessive sugar-coated stories are invariably suspect.

Intuitive, obvious, believable—look for these conditions: If your positioning is in sync with consumers' general beliefs, then it has a better chance to succeed than when it's trying to contrive a make-believe world. Advertisers are regarded to be exaggerators, so some hyperbole is expected, but it cannot go counter to a sense of what seems proportionate and right.

Be driven by potentialities not fears: Too often, positioning calls are not taken for the fear of a looming uncertainty that it might go contrary to what you have decided. When you make choices, uneasiness of the future going contrary to your call will prevail but don't be unduly perturbed. The future cannot be ascertained so not all the variables will be known, but the ones in your view will suffice, if well understood and leveraged.

Previous successes don't safeguard future, nor does previous failure doom future: Positioning is a lot of hard work with diligent consumer listening and taking well-considered calls. Previous experience laden with success or failures can repeat if it's led by rash decision-making. Let every experience be an objective assessment of how well and uniquely you are addressing a consumer need, sticking to the fundamentals of marketing.

Sift the trends from fad: For taking long calls on positioning, it's important that a flighty consumer fad is not understood as a lasting trend, nor should a trend based on a fundamental change in consumer orientation be undermined as a mere fad. Positioning decisions last long so enough care should be taken to unravel the enablers and disablers of trends, to avoid falling into the trap of creating obvious me-too's excited by a prevailing uptick in consumer need. Trends take time to develop and hence, get a good understanding of the pace of change before you build that in your brand positioning.

The above is a watch-out catalogue. Positioning is subtle and subjective therefore guarding one's brand from the usual failures and understanding the requisites of success can go a long way in entrenching positioning.

Measuring personification

How do we know if we have positioned our brand well? Are there some metrics to evaluate that? Unfortunately, no. While a steady increase in revenue and profitability is a good surrogate, it may not be enough or definitive. Since it's a subtle science, we can only eke out some consumer responses to understand how we are being perceived and match that with our intention of positioning. Some qualitative techniques used to measure the result of positioning are as follows:

Personification study encompasses identifying unique attributes of a brand and describing them in terms of personality traits of human beings. Cheetos may be seen as clever and conniving, whereas Lehar Bhujia may be seen as a conservative middle-class person. Pepsi may be seen as a young start-up entrepreneur and Coke may be seen as a dependable marriageable groom. These seemingly innocuous descriptors turn out to be good surrogates of how consumers are decoding our brand upon continuous exposure of our brand messages. A coherent and desirable image shows success; the lack of it portrays schizophrenia in positioning and communication.

Sometimes, if the image lacks sharpness, then you need to tweak communication and brand messaging to call out those traits which set aside the old image to pave the way for the new. If a Sprite personality test throws up a regular guy in college, you need to significantly amp up the cheekiness of the protagonist to make a corresponding impact on the brand. Likewise, if the image shows a reckless guy with poor social affiliation, then creatives have to mellow its edginess suitably to bring the personality in sync with brand positioning.

In some cases, the choice may not be easy. Sometimes, the brand ambassador is imparting the brand with the right values even though the gatekeepers of the brand are critical of the brand personality. This is seen in Boost, which is considered to be enterprising and a go-getter loved by kids, even though it's brand ambassador, Virat Kohli, may not be liked universally by moms for being too abrasive.

In this case, the choice is made in favour of a polarizing persona of the celebrity because it benefits the brand image suitably.

Collages are another technique to capture the brand's world with telling images. In this, consumers are brought into a central location and given magazines and random pictures to make a collage of a brand that best describes their feeling for it, sometimes annotated and later described by them to qualitative researchers. *Metaphors and analogies* may also be deployed to describe a brand in another similar technique to capture the essence of a brand in the consumer's eyes. Doing a comparative collage of brands helps one acquire a surrogate perceptual map of your brand's position versus others.

Some agencies also use projective techniques (meant to elicit response with a provocative trigger) like writing an *obituary* or *matrimonial* or making *brand marriages* to get into the consumer's mind, where detailed diagnostics are required to fix a brand or where consumer response is not easily elicited.

Having laid the foundation of the brand with an informed call on positioning, the time has come to put our best foot forward towards the consumer with communication that reflects the essence of positioning, to bring the desired change in consumer behaviour towards one's brand.

Week 11 and 12

How Do I Communicate with Her?

At this point, it's good to do some stock-taking. We have done well so far in ticking the following in the onboarding checklist: Business and brand orientation, expectations alignment with the boss, cultural understanding of the organization and striking cross-alliances with people. It's time to take a break to develop the skill that brand managers must have: being creators.

Managerial skill: become creators

Marketers are expected to inspire consumption with new promises to their consumers. The premium placed on newness makes them very dependent on the right side of the brain to constantly espouse new ideas. What others haven't done but you can bring to the world, if done consistently, becomes the biggest asset of a company as it differentiates it from the pack.

Creators, or people who innovate at the drop of a hat, are highly valued people in marketing. They can bring about changes in ways that ordinary folk cannot even comprehend and since the prize of consumer loyalty goes to one who delights consumers the most, creators become very critical in staying ahead in the game of delighting consumers.

Are you creative by nature? You probably should have a good idea of that already. If you are, then let your creative juices flow; marketing is as creative as business gets. If not, find someone who can do it for you, since it's not easy to acquire this talent. A few things you could do, however, to positively impact your work with this elusive gift of nature are listed below:

- Seek alternatives: Don't let the first idea, the optimum plan or consensus drive you into complacence. Look for ways to crack the stereotypes and look beyond seemingly efficient solutions for new ways to do things. You may not always have a better alternative to the one on the table but that should not deter you from attempting one. Creativity is unusual, defies predictability and favours constant seeking over certainty. In time, you will realize that even if you posed an alternative that worked once in ten times, it's worth it. Gradually, the percentage of success would improve, ingraining you with this unique quality.
- Enrich perspective: Creativity comes from joining the dots in new ways between ostensibly unrelated variables. The more you open yourself to areas that are not immediately related to your work, the more likely you are to surprise yourself with new ideas. Music, visual art, theatre, cooking, sports . . . follow what you will, even archaeology if you like. Our mind has a way of enriching our thinking when it strays in ways that we will never understand. But for that, take it out for long walks in newer and different ways. Lateral thinking will follow, but you need to let the mind wander and make its own conclusions, almost unconsciously. Learn to let go before you take charge.
- Drop your guard: When you attitudinally seek alternatives and allow your perspective to be enriched, you have to learn to drop your guard. Don't restrict the mind with such rigid frameworks of time and process that creativity is stifled below it. Just cultivate the open space for new ideas to take root

without judging too early and discarding them. If you are initially embarrassed of making a fool of yourself with half-baked ideas not consonant with your image, then practice in your mind and only open up with your ideas in less heavyweight situations. Gradually, as you acquire confidence, you can drop your guard in more consequential meetings and surface spontaneously with ideas that can be made sense of because you will have learnt the art of thriving in ambiguity and shaping things in mid-air from nothing. Creativity has finally come home to roost. Celebrate.

Now let's jump straight into one of the most creative aspects of marketing that deals with communicating with consumers.

Let's get talking

Having done the back-end work of knowing the consumer, it's time to talk to him. Time to communicate. The best of marketing comes to those who bear the responsibility of knowing the consequences of their communication. That leads them to doing all the homework of each step so when the final word is spoken to the consumer, it's well considered. But before understanding the best steps to powerful communication, understanding the mistakes we often make will help us create a foolproof framework.

Communication Errors

What is it? The story is not clear to the consumer. The whole advertisement is played out and you don't know what was the problem in the first place and what solution the brand was offering.

Then comes the next worst thing, where you don't know what problem is being solved. The brand preens in its glory bereft of a context. Consumers register the name of the brand, if at all, but do not have the faintest clue of what it does since its poorly referenced.

In some cases, the problem is understood in detail but you don't understand how the brand is answering it. Or if the brand is answering it, you don't know how it is connected to the problem. Here the opportunity is clearly for the brand to explain what it is and how it's connected to the issue.

What does it do? You have cases where the problem and the answer are not equally matched, meaning you either feel the solution is too small for the problem or it's too big. For instance, getting antibiotics with the first brush of winter is unreasonable, or just putting a mild toilet cleaner for a heavily used toilet is the other extreme of unevenly matched problem and solution.

How does it do it? Also, there are advertisements where the benefit is either not clear or not promising enough to attract the consumers. This could be due to the benefits not being spelt out clearly enough or not being attractive enough, so consumers are neither drawn nor interested.

So what? Finally, there is one where everything happens: problem explained, brand introduced, benefit explained, but the creative is so downright boring that consumers stand completely unmoved as though asking us, "So what's it in for me, why should you bother me?", or may even get repelled from the brand rather than drawn to it. The four types of errors absolutely necessary to avoid are shown below:

Figure 8.1: Communication errors

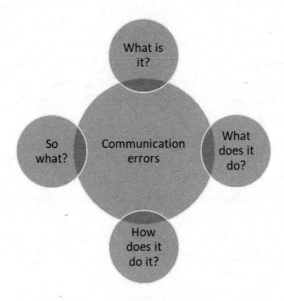

These seem like basic mistakes, leading one to wonder how such mistakes can happen in spite of the experience of a large number of people. Well, that is the reason for it. As stakeholders increase and people with specialized skills step in, integrating their viewpoints into a 30-second creative turns out to be a superhuman challenge.

To avoid this, a bit of academic pretension is permitted here. We have to look at the development of communication from what happens upstream first and then get to work. For this, one needs complete clarity and consensus amongst the client and the agency. Without that, getting an impactful communication is merely left to chance or to someone's strong intuition.

Often there is confusion about the business objective, the marketing objective and the communication objective. All these need to speak to each other and flow logically from one step to another, otherwise a muddled-up approach will confound the consumers more than the internal stakeholders. The business objective states the company's objective, the marketing objective addresses the consumer's need and the communication objective, based on the above two, spells out the intent of speaking to the consumer.

Hence, if a firm has to grow revenue (business objective) by launching washing machine-friendly detergent powder that can optimize washing with machines for the urban consumer (marketing objective), then it must raise awareness of the benefits of this specialized offering versus the general-purpose washing powder (communication objective). The details of this step-by-step approach, starting from the top of the business, ensure effective communication, getting results which are in sync with the business expectation and marketing needs.

Figure 8.2 Objectives cascade

Business objective	What's the company plan?
• Pertains to growth (topline) or profitability (bottomline)
• Stated in market share also
• Delves into utilizing available resources for cashing in on emerging opportunities

Marketing objective	What consumer need is being addressed?
• States what need will be satisfied and why
• how it Is differentiated over competition

Communication objective	How do we want the consumer to react?
• Specifies consumer reaction: awareness/consideration/trial/loyalty/advocacy
• Leads to brand recall and over time, brand equity

At this point, we need to get back to our Need-Want-Barrier/Benefit-Demand (NWB/BD) pathway and solve this with brand communication that operates at a layer below this pathway. Since communication is like telling a story, we have to make a brief that explores all these in detail to create a riveting story.

Communication brief for compelling story-telling

Our NWB/BD gets the following enabling steps under which we need to build on linearly to develop a compelling story with none of the mistakes that we discussed before.

Figure 8.3: Communication structure

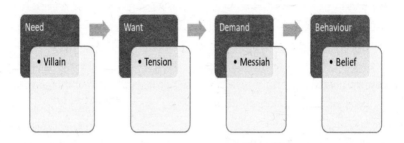

Villain (Need): Fundamentally, consumers seek something because they are deprived. If not, they would never bother to look at you because there are bigger problems in life that keep them busy. So, a marketer's first job is to look for a need and then go deeper to understand how deep is the deprivation. If the deprivation is narrow, brand solutions are not going to be heard. If they are deep, then the brand must claim to satisfy a substantial amount of the deficit that consumers are feeling in their life. If there is no deprivation at the start, marketers should either abandon the idea or try to create a fiction of one (which is difficult, contrived and perhaps short-lived). Without the deprivation at the core of a communication, advertising will just not work.

It's like the villain in the story without whom the protagonist has no role, nor is his success meaningful. The more powerful the villain, the more desirable and bigger becomes the hero. Poor creatives don't establish a villain. Strong creatives elaborate this well.

So, agency and client must write together the real deprivation in the market and deepen with some permissible exaggeration the extent of what consumers are losing out on. For example, there is poor connectivity which leaves you disconnected with the world, there is poor nutrition which can severely undermine the quality of life, there is poor grooming which can impact your chances for success in this world. Notice the deprivation is there, but for communication it has to be extended to highlight its impact on a consumer's life and convert into a need that consumers may have felt so far but now, cannot afford to ignore any longer.

Tension (Want): So if there is a deprivation or a villain and therefore a legitimate need, why isn't the consumer using the options available to satisfy themselves? It's because the competitor categories or products are not fulfilling the deficit caused by the depression sufficiently. Only a part of it is fulfilled, which is not enough when consumers are asked about the level of satisfaction. This is because the deprivation is misunderstood by the manufacturers, leading to inadequate products or there isn't enough partnership between consumers and manufacturers to resolve the deprivation. Or there could be fundamental blocks like poor accessibility (due to availability or pricing) or lack of user-friendliness, which makes it practically difficult to realize the intended benefits.

Now we have opened a gap that paves the way for a story. There is tension in the existing landscape because the villain is walking free and his adversary is not matching up. Without a gap, the story is just not real because you haven't walked in the consumer's shoes to reflect her frustrations, nor does it raise expectations of the consumer for the next step.

Good communicators always look for the gap that leads to tension. This either allows them to directly or indirectly berate competition as being inferior or, in some cases, enables a brand to empathize with the consumer by being very close to her and solving the problem for her. For instance, the lack of miscibility is the reason the gap exists in the dairy whitener category when a wife wants to make a perfect cup of tea, or the mosquito repellents are not effective in killing mosquitoes but leave the beneficiary sleepless suffering because of an odious smell. Or the car looks great, drives well, but comes with a huge service cost that makes it prohibitive (the insight for Skoda).

Without identification of a gap, the story will just lack the tension or the climax to prep the consumer for the entry of the messiah to redeem their miserable lives. Without tension, the creative will fail to create the edge-of-the-seat excitement on the consumer's side for the introduction of your brand.

Messiah (Demand): Now that the deprivation or the villain is established and a gap has been opened citing the inability of the existing options to service the consumer's need, thereby creating tension, it's time to convert the want of the category into the inescapable demand of the brand, by bringing in the messiah or the brand. This appeals to consumers in two ways:

-   Functional benefit: which details what problems will be allayed in a tangible way, like the indulgence of taste cravings, elimination of headache, or adorning well-fitting jeans
-   Emotional benefit: the resultant feeling of pleasure that is invariably associated when a functional need is satisfied.

What is critical to remember is that the story is well told when the solution is in the air before the brand walks in. This way, the brand becomes a very fitting saviour without any hard-selling. Just as the villain is a monster and the hero must be a superhero to get the audience clapping in happy acceptance, so also the tension we create must justify the entry of the brand with its offer customized for the problem.

However, at this point, consumers are not seeing the brand but the solution because we have defined the problem so well that the answer is very apparent. The job now is to build the logical RTB or Reason To Believe to make your brand the best choice for the problem at hand. Thus, a clear RTB such as Vitamin D in milk to support the growth of bones, or a double-sided camera to take selfies from both sides, or a mobile service that works in the remotest of locations because of widespread connectivity needs to be brought out.

In other words, you make your brand a natural hero, a much-awaited messiah because he has all the answers that the problem requires to allay the tension of the consumer. If the problem-solution fitment is good, consumers will be clapping even before the final blow to the villain is dealt because they are expecting nothing but success. This is the power of a story well told, building the right highs and lows.

An additional point is that, if your story has gone down well, you can bring the hero's side-kick, like Robin is to Batman, to further thrill the consumers. Thus, the repeated power failures, justifying the in-built inverter of an air-conditioner or the inability to apply oil to the root of each hair being tackled by the unique comb-like applicator of Indulekha oil that reaches the root of every hair. These ancillary features, apart from the central RTB, establish the primacy of this offer over others.

Another thing to note here is that the benefit must be clearly stitched to the brand purpose (more on this in the next chapter) or the philosophy why the brand exists in the first place at the consumer's service. The closer and more seamless the relationship between benefit and brand purpose, the more durable and endearing becomes the brand communication. Marketers who excel in crafting power brands constantly work on a perfect flow from villain to tension to messiah to strengthen their brand's relevance.

Belief (Behaviour): The ultimate purpose of all communication is to bring about a change in the behaviour of consumers in favour of the brand. Hence, it's important to capture the benefit into an experience of the user so that the belief in the brand is strengthened. It's very important to show the experience of the user in all creatives. This is the only way a potential consumer will be given a tangible end-to-end view of what will happen to him should he embrace the brand. Many creatives miss this aspect and lose a happy end to the story that is an absolute must to close the loop and leave the viewer or the consumer feeling happy, assured and empowered.

For this to happen, the experience of the brand should be written in detail at the brief stage itself: the sumptuous consumption of food, the confidence on being dressed well, the happiness in seeing one's house walls painted and envious neighbours. These are not to be taken for granted since it propels the consumer to embrace the brand and take action, and build a long-term belief in the brand based on joyous association.

Also, it anticipates and helps consumers reinforce this experience as their own experience after consumption. It's easy for consumers to align with a world-view that is imagined by the advertisers for them rather than create their own because consumers either lack the time or cannot imagine the benefits as well as the advertisers can. And here is where the lure of the advertising works best: it creates a make-believe world that end-consumers want to join happily. Some consumers may not be convinced, but the majority will find the projected behaviour agreeable (assuming the product delivers), creating a belief about the brand that will build loyalty over time.

Hence, brands that have elaborate ritual of consumption with telling images of what happens during and post consumption build far more stickiness than those who make a promise and walk away without depicting the full glory of the brand experience. Picture the lip-smacking consumption of Amul, the elaborate world of Titan, the indulgence of Cadbury's Dairy Milk, and the importance of showing the post consumption experience becomes clear.

Brands that fail to do so create the lethal error of 'So what's in it for me?' This question becomes redundant.

Once villain-tension-messiah-belief are written, one needs to add the communication objective and we are ready for the 'Big Idea'.

Communication objective: This connects back to the overall aim of writing this brief. The communication objective is usually one of three kinds:

- Create awareness of the brand proposition
- Spur trials or adoption of the brand
- Reinstate brand loyalty and win more consumers for the brand

Depending on the stage of the brand life cycle (referred to earlier) or the strategic direction chosen by the brand, the above can be spelt out as the clear objective of the communication. Back in the day, people would insist that this should be SOCO (Simple Overriding Communication Objective), thereby forcing the client to focus on the one thing that needs to be achieved from the many. Multiple messaging invariably leads to noise, disabling consumers from picking up the primary signal in a message.

If all the above steps are taken, then we move to what is called the 'Big Idea', the crisp expression of the brand message that would trigger great creatives. Very often, this is the basis for the fine-tuned creative expression or may even mirror it, if it's well-written.

Big Idea

What are examples of a big idea? Below are a few that we have chosen to help you understand the commonalities underlying these great examples.

- Nike: To bring inspiration and innovation to every athlete in the world (from Nike's perspective, if you have a body, you are an athlete).
- Facebook: Empower people to share and make the world more open and connected.
- Amazon: A place where people can come and discover anything to buy.
- Google: The world's information organized so it's universally accessible and useful.
- Snickers: Hunger changes the core of who you are.
- Parachute: Giving everyone a chance to groom, beyond themselves.
- Pepsi: Giving youth the confidence to stand for and live for what they believe in, notwithstanding the world.
- Britannia: Creating healthy food that enriches body and soul.
- Dettol: To assure protection against outside threats to physical well-being.
- Johnson and Johnson: A mother's partner in her infant's growth, in all ways.
- LG: Enhancing life with easy and reliable tools for good living.
- Mentos: Spark new ideas even where it's least possible.

If you evaluate these, then what sets them apart? They are first centred on the product experience so that however far the idea pans out, it still stays rooted in the product truth. Then, it has an ambitious view to embrace their target audience in a way that enhances their life. Google, Nike, J&J, LG—all of them have the desire to influence humanity at large with the offer. At first, it may appear to be advertising hyperbole, but gradually, their range of products and services starts to reflect all of that and build credibility. In the long term, they become owners of that idea, however loftily it's conceived. In that sense, big ideas embrace the biggest and the smallest aspect of the offer in one breath: from small little functionalities to the biggest impact on human lives. And somehow that doesn't seem odd. Finally, big ideas tend to be anti-status quo. They seem to promise a world that fundamentally stands altered when it's touched with the brand experience and in doing so, they promise a better world for the consumer through the lens of the brand.

From all of this, it appears that big ideas have to start small but end big. But if the creative expression is not a faithful representation of the intent of the big idea, this can stay in corporate offices. But these big ideas have inspired great creative expressions like 'Just do it' for Nike, 'You're not you when you're hungry' for Snickers, 'Eat healthy, think better' for Britannia, 'Life is Good' for LG, 'Dimag ki batti jala de' (lights up your mind) for Mentos or the latest 'Har ghoont mein swag hai' (swag in every swig) for Pepsi.

So how do you convert a big idea into a creative expression? Creative expression is the final consumer-facing expression of the big idea. It can often be the big idea itself or may be crafted more crisply for better comprehension and noticeability, evoking a stronger reaction. It's often expressed in the brand taglines.

Unfortunately, creativity cannot be typecast. In fact, it's contrary to standardization since it smacks of newness that old stereotypes completely lack. However, looking at the famous creative expressions that are usually advertising taglines, we can unravel some secrets of this last leap. Needless to say, this has to be preceded by the rigour of briefing and the big idea. Here is what makes great creative expression:

Human truth: For the creative expression to ring true, it must have an element of human truth. That gives it an instant connection with the listeners and also imparts it long memorability. The truth can be overtly stated or it may gleam through, but if it's well conceived and expressed, it will not fail to show. Think about 'Just do it' which intuitively decries the human tendency to keep thinking, at the cost of action. Or Apple's 'Think Different' which hits at the widespread prevalence of everyone reflecting sameness in their thinking. Or closer home, Asian Paints' 'Har ghar kuch kehta hai', meaning every house has a story to tell, brings out the human truth that you can look at a home to know the family that lives within. When creative expressions touch a human truth at the core or even in passing, consumers recognize themselves in it and this intimacy that is created between the brand and the consumer brings the message home.

Human behaviour: Like the above, it goes one step further to reflect what we do when we are in a particular state of mind, experiencing an emotion. 'Finger lickin' good' of KFC cues this planet-truth that if we like some food, we protract the experience by licking those fingers which last held the food to smack of whatever is left. Sometimes you can ride on a human habit to entrench your brand. KitKat celebrates the human desire to take a break from tiring activities and make it worth your while. Hence its tagline 'Have a break, have a KitKat' resonates as much in the past of the consumers as in their future.

Product-centricity: Sometimes it pays to put your product right in the centre of the creative expression or a subtle hint of it, but either way, the product is very much at the core of the thought. Coke's 'Open happiness' is an example of how the uncrowning of the classic bottle cues the oncoming of happiness, in a subtle way. Or 'Amul doodh peeta hai India' is very reminiscent of the self-bleating Dunkin' Donuts line 'America runs on Dunkin', or Thums Up's 'Taste the thunder' works perfectly if the product claim is well matched with the sweeping consumption of the product. Another example is Disney's 'The happiest place on earth' or BMW's proud but incontrovertible 'The ultimate driving machine' or IBM's 'I think, therefore IBM'. If you are towering in stature, go ahead and occupy the pedestal.

Empowerers: Some taglines do an amazing job of creating a world of possibilities for their patrons that not only makes them feel good about who they are now, but also inspires the imagination of future possibilities. Such taglines fly with ease as consumers find a crutch of good living difficult to refuse. L'Oreal's 'You're worth it' does a terrific job in imbuing its users with great self-confidence. Burger King's 'Have it your way' urges you to exercise your power.

Standoffish: Sometimes it pays to confront the prevalent idea (it may be a competitor's or a prevailing fad or trend) and pose your brand's view as a counterpoint. Like 7Up's 'The Uncola' or Pepsi's 'The choice of new generation' or M&M's counter to the category of chocolates through their proposition 'The milk chocolate—melts in your mouth, not in your hands'. Or, in a clever way, you approach the brand from the other end of benefits that brands bring and introduce yourself like, 'There are some things money can't buy. For everything else there's MasterCard.' Or the totally counter view of Surf 'Daag achhe hai', which makes a virtue of dirtying up on the road to life-long learning.

Benefactors: Some taglines scream the benefit the brand brings and become instant benefactors for the consumers. Yellow Pages' 'Let your fingers do the walking' is a clever expression that cues the ease of fishing out your contacts without ending up with sore heels.

Heartwarmers: Some are downright simple, sometimes unabashedly brand forward but whatever they do, they win hearts instantly. For instance, Yahoo's 'Do you Yahoo!' or Rice Crispies' 'Snap, crackle, pop', expressing the product experience, are examples of these simple heartwarmers.

World view espousers: These cue the product as much as the philosophy. For instance, Sprite 'Clear hai' cues not only for the product's clear lemon as a counter to all other high decibel drinks but also brings out its philosophy of effective simplicity over convoluted approaches to life's everyday problems. Or Kurkure's 'Tedha hai par mera hai', which cues the product's unconventional but endearing take on life. Or Lakme's 'Reinvent' which is as much about cosmetic changes with the brand as an exhortation to recast oneself in new ways.

Unless the tagline has a deep association reflecting human realities and it is seated in the core of the brand's experience, creative expressions don't last long. On the contrary, when they do, they multiply a brand's recall and even determine its future journey as consumers stand in its endorsement.

We have seen the framework of communication all the way down to its creative expression. Now let's take a look at one real-life example to see how communication has been developed over the years, reflecting changing times, making it a cult brand.

Communication journey of a brand: case study of Horlicks

Horlicks has been through various upturns and downturns in the last decade or so. For one of India's iconic brands with a huge responsibility to nourish children during their formative years, and to adults who have grown up on the health food drink as a nutrition staple, the challenge for the brand team to keep the brand relevant constantly for a wide spectrum of population is significant. Let's walk down the brand communication journey to understand the application of our framework in a real-life context.

Horlicks, which came to India with the British army at the end of World War I, soon become a favourite dietary supplement for upper and middle-class Indians. Today it is a mega brand with consumption spanning from toddlers to the ageing population. It was marketed as 'The great family nourisher' for a long time and became India's favourite milk modifier (though some people have it with water also, as it was initially advertised) with its trademark malted taste. However, by 2003 the brand diversified with new tastes of vanilla, chocolate and elaichi (cardamom) to cater to its ever-increasing consuming base. Not only that, it has now diversified into distinct offerings for its diverse audience—there is Junior Horlicks, Mother's Horlicks, Women's Horlicks and now, Horlicks Protein Plus. Each of these variants come with their respective communication, but the big challenge is always to put out that umbrella communication for Horlicks which speaks to mothers who are anxious to resolve the need of their child's nutrition.

The communication of 'The great family nourisher', its positioning plank, went through many modifications while retaining its core essence. This was a result of plateauing sales at various points, as the brand matured in its product life cycle, arguing for reasons to increase consumption.

In 2006, based on a consumer insight, the lack of assured nutrition (villain) was felt to be a pressing need. Many players, including Complan and Protinex, talked about growth, but none were able to absolutely quantify how much, how soon. The Horlicks team found this unique opportunity (tension) to reintroduce their product. Now, if they could fix the benefits with a clear RTB, then they would secure consumers' confidence from a functional standpoint and even extend an emotional assurance to the mother as the great family nourisher that the Horlicks brand always stood for.

Moreover, if the experience of the users of the brand was also integrated, post usage, the behaviour of buying Horlicks amongst both users and non-users (who could now be appealed to) could be converted into a life-long belief. This would arrest the dropping sales and equity of the brand.

From this emerged the big idea: 'With Horlicks, your child can be ahead of others' which turned into the sharp, hard-hitting product promise: *'Taller, Stronger, Sharper'* based on clear clinical trials that brought out the difference on these parameters amongst kids who had Horlicks versus a control sample of kids who didn't.

The result was an outstanding success. Equity scores on trust, love, 'for me' and assurance of nutrition moved up just as the sales started to inch northwards, pinching share from unwary competition with a clear message of product superiority.

But a brand like Horlicks, built on huge consumer empathy, would have lost out if emotional appeal was not sufficiently captured in brand communication. To bring the fun back to the proposition of growth, was conceived a campaign whose creative expression or brand tagline was the wonderful phonetic delight: *'Epang, Opang, Jhapang'*, meaning nothing but signifying a whole lot of unbridled fun.

The spontaneous ecstatic consumption of the products in multiple forms made this one of the most memorable campaigns of the time. In the middle of the fun was layered the message of nutrition, fresh from the assurance of nutrition from the 'Taller, Stronger, Sharper' campaign, assuring the mother of the great nourishment of Horlicks. Not only was the brand essence kept intact but the product's emotional quotient of assured growth was incremented with unbounded happiness. Staying in touch with the consumer's evolving needs and reflecting both emotional and functional benefits, the brand was able to sustain its belief and prevent lapsage to competition for some time.

In 2007, the brand infused a figment of topical need by siding with the moms and the kids to overcome the fear of exams. Horlicks' consumption is known to increase during stressful academic times when mothers want quality nourishment to ease the enervating study hours. The *'Exam ka bhoot bhagao'* campaign was brought to life to reflect and assuage consumers' frayed nerves with some success. The campaign gave the brand a stature ahead of its rivals since it constantly mirrored its consumers' concerns and allayed them successfully.

Till 2012, some more campaigns followed, interspersed with the 'Taller, Stronger, Sharper' campaign but its newness and therefore, the credibility was beginning to wane. None of the campaigns that came in the intervening period had the innocent but compelling endearing quality of 'Epang, Opang, Jhapang'. Therefore, it was time to refresh the function and emotional hook of the brand to appeal afresh to a constantly changing lot of consumers especially at the critical recruiting age of 8-12 years..

From this situation was born the next milestone: The '5 signs of growth'. Mothers were looking for more visible signs; competition had upped the ante with equal, if not similar strident claims; and if the 'Taller, Stronger, Sharper' campaign was based on science, there was need for revalidation of that with fresh growth indices. The campaign was launched with a full media thrust, as Horlicks typically does, dominating share of voice through and through. The science was further bolstered by another scientific crutch of 'Nutriabsorb', which highlighted not just the superiority of the ingredients but also their higher bioavailability.

Falling in love with the functionality messaging of the brand, the teams continued to belt out more salvos on similar lines. In 2015 followed the 'Food science' story, quickly followed up by the creatives on 'Immunity' in 2016. The result of this clinical narrative started to show as the benefit of the brand became unidimensional, losing its humanness and with it the strong kid-appeal that has always been the hallmark of this very attractive brand.

During 2014–16, the volumes stagnated and in a category which was growing over 7 to 8 per cent per annum, market share loss became a reality. Penetration of the brand, which as we discussed earlier is an absolute must for mega brands such as Horlicks, took a dip with HHP data showing a loss of 100 bps in the period 2014–16 (MAT data) from 14.7 to 13.7 per cent. A clear alarm for a cult brand like Horlicks when rival food brands, though in distant categories, were either retaining share or growing it (Maggi, Cadbury's Dairy Milk, KitKat).

So what went wrong? After knowing all the winning moves, how did the bag of tricks to woo the consumer run dry?

When we were on the brand, we analysed the issue on the fundamentals of advertising to come up with a solution that turned the tide in favour of the brand after being in the dark ages for nearly four years.

Horlicks' turnaround story

As has been mentioned previously, we analysed the data extensively, did over a hundred consumer immersions and uncovered the reasons for success and failure of the brand. The trends below were unambiguously spelling disaster.

Figure 8.4: Horlicks' performance

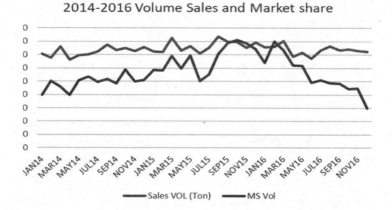

The deep-dive of consumers revealed the following truths that had been lost sight of:

- Nutrition expected of HFD had slipped from being important to negotiable, therefore kids (who always dislike milk) would negotiate their way out since the brand was losing appeal for them. The figure below indicates the declining importance of nutrition. In the cluster approach, we found that milk, fruits, grains and pulses comprised critical nutrition while dry fruits and eggs comprised important nutrition. HFD, which was earlier part of important nutrition, had slipped to negotiable nutrition and got clubbed with the likes of juice and biscuits. The task was to bring it back to the consumer consideration of important nutrition and make it more compelling than other options.

- Doing immersion with the mothers, we found that the parenting style was changing subtly but surely. From goal-based pressured parenting there was a move towards more engaging peer-based parenting. The kid was not being browbeaten into submission with things to do and eat, but reasoned and prevailed upon as a close friend. She was also more assured and informed than before, reading up on the net and chatting with her friends on digital media. She was seeking new things and was willing to experiment.

- The child, being a digital native, is now more confident and more ambitious than before. Pester power or their ability to influence purchase of products has increased and they have a definite opinion and influence on things they consume. Finally, there is a greater desire for recognition as opportunities to do well and showcase one's talent have increased.

- In the environment, there is a trust deficit. Food and nutrition are seen with suspicion and nutrition credentials are being questioned with so much doubt, that moms are veering towards wholesome natural foods.

- As the figure below indicates, the scores for drivers of preference for Horlicks had changed in 2016–17 over 2010–11 with critical parameters like health, children pester and scientific credentials taking a significant dip.

Figure 8.5: Brand scores 2010–17

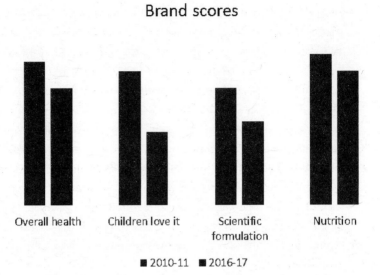

The drop in scores on the science of nutrition (although this was the focus) had a direct correlation with the preference when Horlicks was compared with other brands in the category.

-   Coincidentally, even other brands had shifted to unidimensional functional benefits at this time. Bournvita had shifted to 'Inner strength formula' for stronger bones, muscles and active brain. Complan had shifted to a me-too campaign of two times growth. Boost, another GSK brand which had been built on strong functionality, was focused on three times more stamina. The whole category, resultantly, had become devoid of emotional involvement with consumers as science took centrestage knocking emotion out of the picture. Towards the latter part of the year, however, a smattering of emotional juices started to flow with Bournvita starting 'Tayyari jeet ki' (prepping for victory), a campaign that would set them apart from the rest eventually and Complan brought out the campaign 'Sirf bado nahi, bade bano' or 'Don't just grow, get better'.

Diagnosis: After looking at all the pointers, we came to the conclusion that the real deprivation or the villain of the moment was a soulless interaction with the consumers with everyone making sterile, robotic claims. The reality was that the experience of growth is heavily nuanced with layers of joy and the excitement of growing up which had been missed out. This was the gap for Horlicks to explore as none was resolving the mother's emotional tension of what growth really meant in a holistic way.

The requirement was twofold: mothers needed to be assured of nutrition in a new informative way, but they still needed the emotional companionship of the expert; and kids on the other hand, needed to be won over with a call that would echo with their inner yearning. It was time to turn the indifferent behaviour of the consumers towards adoption of the brand.

Based on this, the creative brief was written. The villain and the tension had to be slain with the right twofold benefit:

- Become a non-negotiable part of child nutrition for the mother with easy-to-understand science, which would also strengthen the nutrition credentials of the brand and give moms a holistic emotional assurance.
- Connect with kids to increase their pester power to bring Horlicks home by reflecting their voice, their contemporary concerns.

This was merged with the brand essence (which is seminal to bring in at this stage) of 'the great nourisher' and the need to balance the emotional and functional tug of the brand. The context of childhood in the current macro-environment with aspirations and opportunities going up in India was looked at.

From this came the big idea:
'Horlicks nourishes the fearless pursuit of hunger'

which was then the basis for the creative expression:
'Badhne ki bhookh'.

This was supported with a unique scientific claim which strengthened the nutrition credentials of Horlicks, giving the reason for its superiority over homemade foods and competition. Horlicks once again became the empowerer to achieve this 'Badhne ki bhookh'.

In a stroke, therefore the brand had taken a vertical lift up:

-   From being a mere fortified drink to a facilitator
-   From treating insecurity as an enabler to making it an enemy (dialling up the negative aspect or the villain to drive urgency in brand consideration, the vital 'tension' that we referred to earlier)
-   From closing gaps in nutrition to opening doors of joys of a possibilities-laden childhood
-   From a nutrition brand for children to a *child's brand* that delivers nutrition

In doing so, we struck the right balance. Turning the indifferent mother and kid into a convinced and demanding duo. From being strong in function with marginal emotions to becoming a robust balance of emotional companion and functional assurance. From deficiency-based storytelling to a saga of success characterized by hope and positivity.

The result was a resounding success. Within a quarter of the launch of the new campaign, all the dipping indices halted and then started to inflect upward, irreversibly. Sales volumes, sales value, market share, brand scores—no parameter stayed untouched as jumps were significant as the figures below indicate.

Figure 8.6: Horlicks volume performance

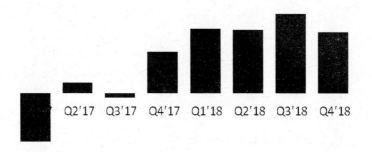

Nielsen Vol Offtake Growth trend

Figure 8.7: Horlicks consideration scores

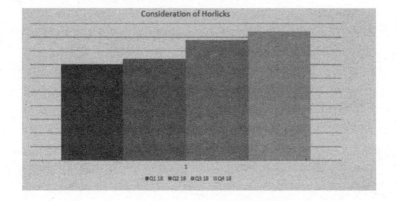

And the biggest delight for a marketer, and the toughest nut—penetration—moved up by 100 bps in one year (2017-18).

On the heels of this success, we mounted another film assuaging mothers and kids during the fearful exam times to strengthen brand connect and further improve sales and brand performance. This will be explored in the chapter on Integrated Marketing.

Communication based on recasting the big idea, therefore, turned the tide for brand Horlicks making it once more the uncontested brand in the pack, driving up category growth. This, in essence, is the power of communication in growing a brand's interaction, and intimacy, with the consumer.

Finally, our brand took a jump up in its purpose and we peaked the consumer interaction with the brand standing for hunger for growth, not mere nutrients. Brand purpose is our next halt to start taking our brand up the perilous but highly rewarding journey of making it a cult or iconic brand.

The Next Three Months

Can I Shape a Cult Brand?

Having slogged for the first twelve weeks in office and made an impact with the right foundations, it's time to start building a long-term successful career in marketing. The next three months are dedicated to equipping you with brand competencies, office art and managerial skills to craft cult brands that people will recognize as your contribution long after you have left.

If you look closely at your style of work in office so far, you would have noticed that, depending on what kind of person you are on the STRIVES framework, you have a tendency to approach every problem from the way you are predisposed.

This is 'tendency bias' or the inherent often unrealized handicap of seeing the situation not as it is but as we are prone to seeing it. Accordingly, even the solutions that we direct to answer the problems are based less on what is required and more by what we can do. Thus, a creator innovates wherever he sees a problem whether the situation requires it or not and a researcher dives deep to unravel the root cause when just simple action may be required. Don't believe it. Take a look at this grid below and ask yourself which tendency you operated from when the situation presented itself in myriad ways.

Figure 9.1: Tendency bias

Situation/ Tendency	Specialist	Team-worker	Researcher	Improviser	Visionary	Executor	Shaper
Finance							
Marketing							
Human resources							
Supply chain							

If you are beginning to realize a pattern to your style, it's a good thing you are self-aware already. Many managers have spent their entire life looking at the world from their tendency and believing it to be adequate when the situation was diverse, offering many avenues for growth. But they could never take off the blinkers of their bias to see the world in a different light than the one cast constantly by their perspective.

Managerial skill: Team worker

At this point, let's look for the team worker managerial skill in you. Or, in your neighbourhood, who you can leverage to build a solid team. How do you spot a team worker; what sets him or her apart?

Team workers inherently love people and their inter-dynamics. They have no favourite nor are they easily put off by people different from them; instead they draw their energy from assembling a motley lot of people on a single canvas. Their joy comes from seeing the varied colours blend together and they go out of their way to be *inclusive*. Team workers are fundamentally good at bringing people together. Whether they use a common goal, a common rival or their charm as the social glue, they seem to operate with great ease in turning surface-heterogeneity into inherent-homogeneity.

What is their motivation? They delight in rallying around a common cause. To them the quality of the cause, or the reason for their affiliation to it is less important than their desire to bring a solution or dispel ambiguity with a purpose for their group. Team workers then go on to allocate responsibilities depending on their assessment of the abilities of people, decide terms of collaboration, fix timelines and then stand back to let group dynamics take over. They are great *enablers* of group functioning, with no hidden urge to lead it. They just like doing it. If members contribute and participate without conflict, their purpose is served; if not, they quickly proceed to work and address the disruption amicably. They are to teams what lubricant is to an engine. They are ubiquitous in the way they get to work in every nook and cranny of a group, but almost inconspicuous since they lack any fixed position or stature.

Many a time when you execute projects of complexity and scale, this attribute becomes imperative. It's more important and effective than overt leadership. So, developing the capability to be inclusive and rally people together is a critical virtue to acquire. If you don't have it, look for someone who exudes these skills effortlessly. This one is absolutely critical.

With that, let's see what keeps marketers up at night: the worry of underperformance or the zeal to create brands that bear marks of consumer's love.

Lure of a cult brand

Everyone wants to work towards creating cult brands or inherit one and make it even more powerful than before. No brand manager worth his salt is content to be an also-ran and the rare who do, have not tasted the high of riding the high horse of a cult brand. Having worked on some, we can testify it's a rush like none other and is a fortune that must visit every professional's life.

So what makes a cult brand? Before we understand how to craft one, let's be clear about the enormity of the task ahead.

Cult brands' DNA

Cult brands show common traits if you read between the love marks that their consumers bear.

High need-satisfaction: First things first. If you want a brand to be a cult, it must fulfil all the functional needs of that category. Your patrons should have no doubt that this is the very best experience they can get from this category. In fact, as we will see later, it goes beyond that, but the journey to consumer ecstasy starts with leaving no aspect of their wish unfulfilled. So, Harley Davidson tops the driving experience on two wheels so much that it makes people embrace the lifestyle that comes with it. Maggi noodles in India set the taste buds on fire regularly and people associate it with phases of their life as though it was a living person. The presence of Dettol imbues absolute confidence in protection from infection in the gravest time of consumers' lives. Apple's phones are as important to you as your closest friends. No wait, it's closer than one's closest friends, as most consumers would testify.

There may be differences in the degree of cult-status but the journey of these cult brands starts when they index on the highest side of the consumer scale of satisfaction in the category they strut in as a leader.

Irreplaceability: Cults are like subscribing to a religion. You don't have two of them. Likewise, cult brands refute replaceability because they knock everything down before cranking themselves up to the highest pedestal of preference. It's either them or nothing. Gillette is the best a man can get, literally. Amazon's replacement is difficult if you are addicted to the click on that universal app. Trademark Beetle is unsurpassed for its look and safety. Body Shop gives an experience that leaves others far behind. If other brands do occasionally replace them, consumers rush back to their cult brand with renewed loyalty—the difference in experience is so palpable and unforgettable. In their sheer dominance of the demand space they occupy, they have a monopolistic grip on their market.

Uniqueness: The sum total of the immersive experience they enthral their consumers with is not possible to replicate. Cult brands with the depth of their benefits, emotional and functional, strike such an inimitable impression that consumers just can't be lured by any me-too's. The experience of a Hummer, the feel of a Patek Philippe may seem to have generic elements to outsiders, but ask their loyalists and they wouldn't be willing to consider any alternatives by a long shot. The appeal of cult brands is built on benefits that are unique for their patrons. Eventually, the unanimity amongst their consumers is strong that they go on to form a community of like-minded loyalists, and fiercely defend their choice to those outside their circle, à la the members of Harley Owners Group.

Essence: Cult brands have a core which is consistently resonant with their target audience. The core of the brand helps the brand call out very unambiguously to the people it's reaching out to, as much as the people reach out to the brand for what it stands for. Thus, if Google wants to organize information for the benefit of the world, people resonate with that vision and constantly turn to its door—a perfect consonance of the need and its corresponding solution. If Nike believes that there is a sportsman in everyone, then quite surely people of all ilks, regardless of their enthusiasm for sports, find common cause in Nike's products. Cult brands have perfect overlap with the needs of their consumers, having understood them to perfection and resolved them better and ahead of others.

The consistency of doing many things around the same essence rather than many things around several essences characterizes cult brands unlike their unsuccessful competitors. They understand that it's better to be everything around one core idea than many things across many core ideas. With such focus, consumer confidence in the ability of the brand to anticipate their needs and solve it for them only goes up with every interaction. By meeting their consumers' expectations, in fact, often shaping them, they are able to turn ordinary interactions with their consumers into relationships of indelible trust.

Heritage: Like exemplary people and formidable nations, cult brands come with a rich saga of struggles and successes in the pursuit of their cause. Typically, it goes back decades, sometimes over a century, bringing out the brand essence showcased in the brand's birth through the vision of the founding fathers. Most global restaurant chains like McDonald's, KFC and Taco Bell play up their humble but well-intentioned origin in their parlours, bringing out their brand character in a subtle way. This historical canvas goes a long way in helping consumers contextualize the brand and build an ongoing association of deep-rooted trust.

As the stories get deeper and more meaningful, the brand starts to take root in consumers' mind and heart. What time does to the quality of relationships, heritage does to the strength of brand connections. Cult brands not only connect deep but also far. So, it becomes important that brands do storytelling consistently so that the connection with history is seamless. How a brand continues to adhere to its core values, what it did and has been doing consistently to support the values, and how it's well equipped to deal with consumers' expectations in keeping with the brand's DNA—these are steps to life-long intimacy.

World-view: Cult brands have a world-view, meaning they interpret the world through the lens of the brand's values and offering. This helps brands connect with the community they originate in and contribute back to it. More importantly, it tells their patrons what philosophy they stand for so consumers can align with the company's vision. The philosophy articulates how it positively impacts the human race towards a larger goal of the planet. It's lofty, often seeming to stand far from the commercial realities of the brand, but it becomes a guiding beacon and a unifying thread for all its activities.

So, Google stands for empowering people by democratizing information, Nike believes that if you have a body, you have an athlete in you, Apple believes in simplifying, thinking different to make a positive impact on people's lives. Sometimes, the philosophy is articulated in the vision, sometimes in the statements of its leaders, or just through what they do with their products and services. But whatever the mode of expression, there is unmistakable consistency emanating from the brand's core essence and purpose.

Empowerment: As a result of all the above, cult brands endow their consumers with tremendous power. From being just recipients of the specific benefits of the brands, consumers of a cult brand eventually turn up enriched much more at the end of the brand interaction. This is because cult brands bring out active participation of the consumers and together with them create a better individual experience for each one. Apple devices, Nike shoes and Amazon shopping are huge enablers to every one of their users in multiplying their potentialities into realities.

It's this power of cult brands to make their consumers a better version of themselves that lets them win evangelists and lifelong ambassadors easily. Consumers identify so closely with the brand that they consider any attack on the brand as an attack on themselves. The downside is that when they are disappointed, they really need to be listened to and pampered. Visualize an irate Apple evangelist and you know the fury of cult followers.

Mystique: When cult brands are completely decomposed threadbare to every element that makes them who they are, an unknown segment remains that defies explanation. You can't point your finger to call out its true nature, nor can others comprehend it if you did try. This ineffable stuff of cult brands is a lot like cult figures. You can analyse their lives, their views, even predict their reactions sometimes, but you can't re-create them. It's something like the secret formula of the classic Coke which remains undecipherable.

From the examples above, it would appear that very few Indian brands have made it to this list of cult brands. It may be because they haven't tried hard enough to embrace the larger life of consumers or haven't given a platform for consumers to get on board with them. Either way, several of our brands lack the respect, trust and love that cult brands elicit.

Here's looking at how to make that happen for the brands at your disposal. A word of caution is that it may be a long haul, perhaps materializing long after you are gone, but unless it gets started, it's unlikely to happen by accident.

For making cult brands, you need from the arguments above the following, with BRAND PURPOSE at the core of the brand. The figure below consolidates what we need to start working on earnestly from today and every day.

Figure 9.2: Cult brand schemata

Brand purpose: Brand purpose or the core of the brand, equivalent to the DNA of a human being, has two parts encoded in it:

- Core values or what is also called brand essence, which justifies a brand's existence in consumers' lives
- Its actions to demonstrate the commitment and impact of its values in consumers' lives. It gives values, a potential idea, kinetic energy to bring brands alive.

Values are defined as principles or standards of behaviour that reflect what one regards as important in life. It's a widely used term every day but for the brand, no less than a person, it connotes what the brand regards to be of utmost importance in doing business. It justifies its everyday endeavours towards satisfying consumer needs, but also links it with a higher order benefit. Those brands that lack the latter run the risk of staying merely transactional with consumers vulnerable to better pricing or promotion lures of their competitors.

This can be simplified further as:

- *What* a brand sells or markets—most consumers will be able to tell being either patrons of it or having heard of it. This is the visible piece, often when it's not even solicited.
- *How* a brand comes to your hand—its making at the back end, its partnership with other stakeholders, the logistics and storage. It may even illustrate its constant research and development to delight consumers ahead of competition. For instance, Ben and Jerry, the ice cream manufacturers, spell out this in their vision: 'We make the best possible ice cream in the best possible way.' Through this, they highlight responsible sourcing covering all aspects of environment conservation. Being transparent and above board for the entire value creation is a great way to transition from a mere 'what-brand' to a 'how-brand'.

- *Why* a brand exists beyond the commercial pursuit—it's the reason why it continues to provide support to consumers, even anticipates their needs before they can express it, and staying continuously invested in servicing that need.

Referring back to our NWB/BD model, brand purpose converts the want of the brand, which can arise from awareness or consideration from advertising, into an unrelenting demand by aligning consumer's want with the brand's capabilities and purpose. Brand purpose then does the critical job of unlocking the barrier to consumption of a category and enables benefits to flow with the characteristic brand's signature.

To build brand purpose, therefore, you must take undertake following steps as an exercise, even if you are unable to execute part or whole of it immediately. Ordinarily, brand purpose can be found reflected within the company's vision or mission. However, if that is not articulated clearly, lacking specificity or direction, then the following steps are recommended: the F-E-R-O inner wheel of brand purpose

- *Functional benefit (F)*: Start from the product's functional benefit. What it does to a consumer sensorially—taste palate, skin, aural, overall well-being . . . nail the specific benefit that consumers palpably feel.
- *Emotional derivative (E)*: Next, take the functional benefit forward by looking at what emotions of consumers it satisfies. We referred to the whole spectrum of emotions in the chapter on needs. Evaluate from consumer feedback, social listening or a dipstick on how consumers feel after interaction with the brand. Happiness, joy, ecstasy, break from monotony, uplifted, recharged, released from depression, self-enhanced, self-actualized . . . the list of human emotions can be explored in depth to arrive at something specific and believable from your brand. Once you have selected it, repeatedly check and refine till you are sure about its uniqueness and believability. Then, make your brand own the reason for that emotional outpouring.

Explain how it unlocks the barrier, paving the way for emotional benefits to flow.

- *Resultant behaviour (R)*: Then, explore what happens as a result of the emotional high that the consumer faces on interacting with your brand. The positive state that it leaves them with must surely impact their behaviour. The brand experience doesn't merely end with the direct consumption but also lingers on in the activities indulged in as a result of feeling the emotional uptick—understanding this differentiation sets the exceptional marketers apart from the usual ones.

- *Opportunities pursuit (O)*: Finally, link this behaviour of the consumer with his pursuit of better life experiences (the ultimate goal for most consumers) and underscore that for the consumers repeatedly so they understand the role of the brand, however small or insignificant initially, having the capability to make big differences to their life. Initially, it may seem incredulous but through consistent storytelling and attuning of your brand's product and services in this direction, these seemingly distant benefits start to make sense.

Figure 9.3: F-E-R-O—inner wheel of brand purpose

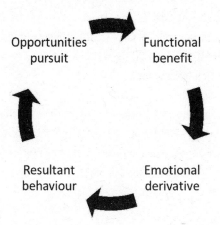

Once you have nailed this F-E-R-O wheel (functional benefit–emotional derivative–resultant behaviour–opportunities pursuit), your brand purpose starts to uncover itself like gold after assiduous panning.

Here are a few examples of this step-by-step approach:

- Use of Glow & Lovely makes me glow (functional benefit), overcoming my physical limitation (emotional derivative), and gives me the confidence (resultant behaviour) to reach out for better life opportunities that I considered impossible (life-linkage).
  o   Brand purpose: Glow & Lovely believes in giving confidence to achieve out-of-reach dreams.

- Drinking Amul milk makes my bones and muscles strong (functional benefit), enhancing my physical being to make me stand out in the crowd (emotional derivative), making me lead in everything I do.
  o   Brand purpose: Amul milk stands for building individuals who will stand out in whatever they do.

- Receiving a Titan watch as a gift, the best in style and elegance (functional benefit), I feel ecstatic (emotional derivative) since my superlative performance is now being recognized.
  o   Brand purpose: Titan reflects and believes in recognizing personal excellence.

The above examples are indicative in nature. However, marketers would do well to use the F-E-R-O wheel to underpin the brand's values and articulate the purpose of their brand so we can lay the foundation of the cult brand.

Heritage:

Cult brands take time to build because trust and veneration emerge only when a brand has tested true over many occasions. But just long-standing performance is not sufficient for someone to be revered beyond reason. It takes peeking into the history of their origin, so their humble but lofty ideal is laid bare for everyone to feel and be in agreement with.

Harley calls out its heritage of world exploration, Oprah's show stands unequivocally for candour, Fabindia celebrates India, Body Shop of Anita Lucia Roddick has been built on fair trade with developing countries and non-testing of ingredients on animals.

Ordinary brands are built on stories; cult brands are built on stories with human values being demonstrated. If you don't have heritage, there is no demonstration of brand purpose. On the contrary, heritage establishes beyond doubt the brand's belief in action, and also its steadfast adherence to that through the highs and lows.

This represents a big opportunity for Indian brands that have just started their march to cultdom. Natural's, the pioneering ice cream from JVPD, Mumbai, has proudly built its story based on ingredients of natural fruits. In parlours, amidst rich canvases of fruits, TV screens play out the painstaking fruit-procuring process underlying their unique ice cream. To lend credibility, only seasonal fruits feature in their range of fresh ice creams. That goes so far as to make its summer fare a hit in cold Delhi also, where consumers have found the story of fruit-indulgence indifferent to weather. This is the power of stories built on heritage.

How do you build stories once the brand purpose is crafted as above? The best stories are built when the three elements of culture, consumer and brand interconnect. In other words, it reflects the brand essence, which is in sync with the consumer's demand and corroborates what the culture of the prevalent time is cueing. We have dealt with consumer demand and brand essence; how do we understand the culture of the times?

For this, we have to delve into the psychology of culture stereotypes and choose the most suitable one. Culture stereotypes as per eminent psychologist Carl Jung are 'universal, mythical characters or concepts that transcend time, culture and geography and reside in humanity's collective subconscious'. If the heritage of the brand is built around a stereotype, it is easily understood and transposed on the consumers because they are already pre-exposed to it and, due to social conditioning, also believe in it. Hence, the task of the marketer is far easier as it's more efficient and effective to ride the powerful tool of popular culture than to make a fresh narrative which has no roots in the collective consciousness of people.

Thus, archetypes are a very powerful tool available in the human psyche to help consumers connect to the brand. While there are many archetypes, they have a few traits in common. These include:

-   A pressing call to address a situation
-   A protagonist gets ready to respond through an ordeal or an initiation
-   A battle ensues that causes a transformation
-   Resolution and the restoration of peace and order

The critical thing in these stories is the enabler who makes this journey possible. This is prevalent in our mythology, our popular culture, even Bollywood. Thus, Ram has the help of Hanuman, Arjun gets the assistance of Krishna, or more recently, Harry Potter gets the help of Dumbledore, or Neo gets the help of Morpheus in *The Matrix*, or Rocky is nudged to greatness by Mickey. Brands can take the role of such enablers if they fit in the popular psyche deftly. Now, let's see what the archetypes are and how some brands have found them their home for building heritage.

Carl Jung has explained 12 core archetypes:

- **Creator**: means if you can imagine something, you must be able to turn that into reality. It takes imagination and creativity and therefore, brands or organizations that foster this amongst their consumers can build on this stereotype. Lego, the toy game for kids, or YouTube, which inspire people to innovate and create their own toys or content is a perfect fitment for this archetype.
- **Lover**: is one who indulges oneself to be physically and emotionally more attractive. The talent of such a person is usually on the side of passion and appreciation of fine things. The brands suitable for this archetype are those that differentiate themselves from other lower-priced brands through refined appeal to a sense of finer things. They appeal to beauty, intimacy and attention to detail, and such brands help people find friends and appreciation as exemplified by L'Oreal and Victoria's Secret.
- **Royalty:** is driven by the idea that power is everything, for which you must have a talent for leadership. Think about the stories of the Godfather, Cleopatra or the Nizam and you understand how they impact popular thinking. This is appropriate of brands where domination and leadership over ordinary brands is important to drive brand preference. Some premium liquor and tobacco brands in India allude to this archetype.
- **Maverick:** believes that rules are meant to be broken. Think of Trump or Virat or Elon Musk and you begin to understand the challengers to the system who ended up owning it. The talent required for this is outrageous outspokenness and a high degree of self-belief. Brands that are trendsetters, going against the system to the extent of establishing their counter narrative, can take the mantle of this archetype. Diesel Jeans, Harley-Davidson and Jack Daniel's are some examples of its adherents.
- **Sage:** believes that the truth will set you free. The talents required of such people are wisdom and intellect. Brands that purport

to empower consumers with tools and knowledge to avoid mediocrity would do well to build on this. Google, Harvard University and somewhat the Isha Foundation of Sadhguru (which also sells merchandise) gravitate towards this popular aspect.

- **Next-door neighbour**: is based on the human value that all people are created equal and so must be the opportunities. The belief is that solid ordinary virtues must be built with a sense of empathy and realism. Brands like Levi's, McDonald's, Ikea or even Big Bazaar in India can leverage this, as they provide solid functional benefits with easy accessibility and affordability for maximum benefit.

- **Victor**: or Hero believes that where there is a will there is a way. Think of Sachin Tendulkar or Arvind Kejriwal, the activist and politician, and your mind starts to conjure images of worth, competence and courage built on doggedness centred on a strong purpose. Brands that show the belief of winning over everyday problems with consistency and outlasting inferior competition through sheer performance are suitable for such a narrative. Duracell, Gatorade, Dettol—these brands show elements of this archetype.

- **Seeker**: believes in breaking barriers and monotony in the pursuit of finding one's answers. Think of *Star Trek*'s Captain Kirk, or Indiana Jones, or Abhimanyu in Indian mythology, and brands that advocate independence, honesty, ruggedness and durability would be candidates for this. The apparel brand North Face, National Geographic or even Aaj Tak channel exemplify 'Seeker'.

- **Performer**: believes in making the most of life since it comes only once. The talent is one of loving fun and simplicity. Visualize Kapil Sharma, or Chandler of *Friends* and you get a space for brands like Sprite or Mentos.

- **Caregiver**: believes in compassion and giving, à la Mother Teresa or Angelina Jolie as a human rights ambassador. Brands that are into sharing, health and caring are ideal. Body Shop or Volvo are good ambassadors and it is potentially a space for Airtel, Fortis Healthcare or Johnson & Johnson to move into.
- **Innocent**: believes in being oneself, blissfully. Think of Tom Hanks in *Forrest Gump* or Aamir in *PK* and you get the sense of satisfaction in being inhered in one's own world. Huggies and Dove suit this well with the innocent charm they exude.
- **Inventor**: the visionary who changes the world with his imagination and grit. Think of Nelson Mandela and Messi, and the talent of imagining and finding win-win solutions comes to the fore. Brands that promise to transform and walk with consumers in their journey even resorting to spirituality to inspire fit this well. Glow & Lovely, Byju's, Anand Spa— these brands, consciously or unconsciously, are building on this stereotype.

We have tried to fit Indian examples in most of these stereotypes while illustrating the foreign ones also. Whether you are managing a global brand or grooming one from the soil, you need to find an archetype that best represents your brand's purpose and the consumer's need it satisfies. Once that is done, build on brand heritage (and even other brand manifestations that we will touch upon next) so consumers see shades of these stereotypes. As the resemblance gets close, consumers will start to understand, accept and even multiply your idea with their imagination, thereby giving the brand substantial roots in local culture and their lives, no less than accepting a family member in your life who you have grown up to trust and be with at all times.

For instance, if you are Haldiram's, then taking the archetype of 'Royalty', you can build on the brand heritage of the best recipes from the historical land of Rajputana, reflecting the choicest ingredients and recipes of royalty. You can create a world rich in taste, texture and aroma brought to every man by trained chefs through multiple parlours at an affordable price, thereby allowing every Indian to live the life of the elusive royalty. Suddenly, the brand acquires roots in the culture and evokes associations far richer than any single brand with any product range can evoke. Consumers on their own will give the brand the vivid colours and textures of the royal families of Bikaner, the multicoloured world of Rajasthan with its rich history. If this is well aligned with the brand purpose, Haldiram's could well be on its way to becoming a giant.

Or, if you are the custodian of Titan Watches, your chosen archetype could be an inventor who innovates within India but shows quality that is internationally acclaimed like Aryabhata, or J.C. Bose, or Wangchuk more recently. Durability, vision, local pride, international acclaim—all these images start to float in your head as you build Titan's heritage as a watchmaker that literally set the clock back on time, recreating quartz watches, overtaking behemoth HMT and then pioneering to create the slimmest watch in the world. The inventor imagery now becomes imbued with national pride and international possibilities, and both patriotic Indians and citizens of the world start to enlist in support of this stereotype. The brand is enriched with local flavour and develops international strides in the same breath by getting a cultural context appropriate to its brand purpose.

You can take any brand and vivify it with the richness of legacy in this way. Try it with Bata, Ola, Flipkart or any other brand and see how you can enrich them by situating them in a cultural context through building heritage.

That takes us to the next steps in building brands: Brand Assets.

Assets: *Star Trek* lives on as much in its story as in its memorabilia. Marvel creates a world in plastic figurines of its heroes that lingers long after the film and comics are read. Disney, built on experiences, defines the city through its landmark theme parks. But brands? Most of them live and die in that little packaging that carried them humbly to their consumer's home. Cult brands act and think differently.

They make a world for their consumers to walk into and lose themselves in. Surrounding their senses, extending into many adaptations and versions, they enthral consumers with their all-embracing offers and services. Apple has created stores that carry the minimalism of its design into retail interactivity for its consumers to get a tactile feel of the brand. Samsung has stores where you see its current and future world unfolding before your eyes with technology that you never thought was possible, even though there is no sale from these stores. Reebok measures your fitness levels and gives you counselling without bothering to sell their sports gear. Why?

Cult brands realize that selling is a smaller and inevitable tail of the consumer interaction, but the real deal is to win over their hearts. That way, not only do consumers buy in large numbers but buy for a lifetime and coax others to buy for you. Cult brands insist on prevailing on your mind for a lifetime, rather than just one time or one unit sale of that product.

Woefully, however, almost all brands offer no immersive experience. There is such a huge opportunity for these brands to take a core idea and multiply its representations to overwhelm the consumers that revenue registers may never stop ringing. How does one convert a single brand logo and a few SKUs into a cult brand? Below is a shopping list that you must look at adding to your brand cart:

- **Packaging**: Move from being the staid packaging design that is usually industrial in nature to more consumer-friendly, contemporary designs in keeping with the brand purpose. Brainstorm in groups on a brand experience and translate that into words and pictures, and hire a design agency to bring out a new design. Then ask yourself where is the brand consumed—

in what format, on what occasions and in what surroundings. Create different packaging designs developing the brand elements (logo, colour, texture) in a consistent way. Change formats and textures of packaging if you have to for being relevant to festivals, social occasions or even customized packs for consumers.

- **Consumption Associations**: What else does the brand connect with in the moment of consumption? Bru is had in a mug, prepared in a certain way, served on a coaster, with friends, in different moods, on the way to office as a recharge, as an evening rewind, to call it a day . . . how many occasions can you think of and where can you put the brand to multiply your assets? Bru mugs, Bru coasters, Bru cup holders, Bru office mugs, Bru mood mugs, Bru party mugs (like beer mugs), Bru decoction. Think of the brand multiplication, think of the sheer ownership of coffee consumption and the brand starts to take fresh wings.

- **Consumption Occasions:** Now that you have somewhat put the brand memorabilia out, can you create occasions that are not usually associated with Bru? Can you develop Bru dispensing machines for home which deliver the experience of a cappuccino with the signature taste of Bru? Can you take that to office also or even on a hike? Can you partner with technology and app guys to give you various other coffee formats using Bru as an ingredient?

Go further and open franchisee operations. While this has commercial challenges and puts you squarely in the middle of a crossfire between Starbucks and Café Coffee Day, even a few of your parlours will go a long way in bringing the brand alive to consumers in an immersive experience. Service opportunities for the brand sorely missed by many product brands as much as service brands miss the retail in-home opportunity for their brands. Consumers consume brands not occasions, but marketers stay closeted in self-created walls, unable to break these false divisions.

The more brand assets you have, the better the visibility and demonstration of your brand's worth to consumers. Look at the rich memorabilia of Pirelli or Harley-Davidson and you can glimpse how far the world of brands can extend. Stopping at mere packaging of a strong brand is short-changing its potential. Consumers are waiting and willing to see their brands represented and available a lot more and marketers block the journey up to the cult brands by failing to listen to consumers.

Before we move to the next step towards cult brands, it is important to remember that in building brand assets, one has to be careful to retain the core of the brand properties (graphics, tonality, texture, voice . . . all its portrayals palpable to the five senses) while multiplying other avenues. This careful balance between continuity and brand consistency will be dealt with further in Integrated Marketing.

World-view: Cults are known for the sway they command over their members with their ideology. Cult brands cannot merely sell products and expect their consumers to root for them if they don't stand for an ideology towards a bigger cause that affects the larger community. So how do you formulate a world-view for your brand so its appeal extends further and wider?

World-view is an extension of the brand purpose. In the F-E-R-O model above, we stopped at 'opportunity pursuit' that the brand allows. Now, we look at what happens when individual consumers are satisfied and its impact at three levels:
- People or the community that the brand serves at large
- Planet where consumers live
- Profit or how the company's generated wealth is put to use for benefitting the above two

As brands expand and their user base becomes substantial, they constitute a community as large as a country. Facebook or YouTube users cover almost 15–20 per cent of the world's 7 billion population and are growing constantly. Google, Amazon, Apple, Coke or closer home, Amul and Tata have consumers who add up to a substantial voice. Willy-nilly these brands are anyway impacting a large number of people with their brand offering. So, it's becoming of them to embrace this responsibility not merely as a consequence of their size but also by deliberate design. And sure enough, this is reflected in their vision if you glance through the vision of iconic brands.

- Google: 'To provide access to the world's information in one click.'
- Instagram: 'Capture and share the world's moments.'
- LinkedIn: 'To connect the world's professionals and make them more productive and successful.'
- Nike: 'To bring inspiration and innovation to every athlete in the world.' Inspired by the founder, Bill Bowerman, who said, 'If you have a body, you are an athlete.'
- Quora: 'Quora connects you to everything you want to know about.'
- Walmart: 'To help people save money so they can live better.'
- Titan: 'We create an elevating experience for the people we touch and significantly impact the world we live in.'

If we further connect back to the NWB/BD pathway, it's clear that each of these companies have unlocked fundamental desires of mankind. Need to know (Google, Quora), need to share happiness (Instagram), need to succeed professionally (LinkedIn), need to live better (Walmart), need to be fit (Nike), need to be emotionally uplifted (Titan): these need-states will give these companies longevity and relevance beyond this century.

The closer to human needs a company gets, the better their chance to appeal not just to consumers but the human beings that they are. In that sense, world-view connects the consumer with the world and allows companies to see their patrons as human beings first and last. The expansion of this scope is bound to reflect positively in their brand image, setting them up on the journey to cultdom.

Planet: When you impact such a large swathe of humanity, the positive influence on the planet cannot be far behind. Companies that have taken this on in their business vision are far more likely to win consumers' endorsements as the need to know about companies' commercial operations increases. In fact, companies and brands are making their practices more transparent as an essential part of winning consumer trust. Lately, a lot of brands have taken to *cause marketing*, linking their brand with larger environmental concerns like plastic disposal, global warming, rainforest depletion and protection of wildlife.

Many brands have not been able to clean up their internal stables to make claims like these but smaller, enterprising brands that have done so are rapidly garnering consumer support, and their equity is becoming more formidable than the bigger players in that category.

Some good examples of world-view based on protection of the planet are Apple and Tata's whose statements vividly demonstrate the inclusive world-view they hold about the world.

- Apple :'To ask less of the planet, we ask more of ourselves.'
- Tata (the text appears in the Mission of the Tata Group): 'To improve the quality of life of the communities we serve globally through long term stakeholder value creation based on Leadership and Trust.'

Profit: What companies do with the net profit they generate is often a matter of interest for many. When companies communicate their intention to contribute a part of their income for the welfare of the community, it removes all suspicion of opportunism and profiteering that people may harbour, ushering in instead, respect and love.

Doing thus, companies cover the journey of profit, people and planet to enter a circular loop of value creation, changing the current 'linear' model of create–utilize–waste. Sustainability, it hardly needs saying, becomes a natural offshoot.

Brands that feed back to the communities through what is commonly called corporate social responsibility win hearts and stamp an indelible mark on their existing consumers as well as additional ones who troop into the brand's world willingly.

So, if you write the world-view of the brand, you need to supplement the F-E-R-O with W or world-view. As an example, Amul fulfils nourishment needs (F), giving me a sense of well-being (E), giving me the confidence to reach out (R) for my life's dreams (O), thereby contributing to the making of India through its inspired citizens (World-view). Most brand purposes can be extended to include world-view. But once that is done, brand managers should commit themselves to building towards that with all their marketing activities, from communication to innovation to cause marketing, day after day for years.

Empowerment: Cult brands are eventually owned by the consumers, not by marketers. This takes as much courage as imagination.

When a brand is built, it speaks to consumers but as it develops, the consumers start to talk back. Their experiences, their expectations, their frustrations and joys even on things unrelated to the brand directly. This is not the moment to shirk back in horror but to welcome it. It implies that consumers see the brand as a close friend, making the communication a two-way street. And when relationships get deeper, consumers start to take liberties, like any human interaction, and even speak up for the brand as brand owners and custodians. At this point, brand managers need to step back and let consumers take charge. The downside is that sometimes the narrative from the consumer's mouth may not be entirely to the liking of the brand manager, but the upside is that now consumers are working for the brand, not the brand for the consumers. This is the time to celebrate. The evolution of the brand from being a transaction to a love mark of the consumer is as shown below.

Figure 9.4: Empowerment evolution

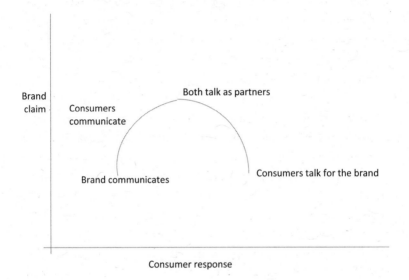

From the above, it's clear that when brands do well, they have to eventually talk less because their brand evangelists do the talking. From being the provider of service and products, the brands transition to being the platform or the opportunity for the consumers to talk. And this works just as well because if the communication is built on brand purpose, it's the same thing, except the communication from consumers has much more authenticity and goes a long way in enlisting other consumers like them. This truly sets up a blistering pace for the brand to build in scale and stature.

The growth of Facebook, Instagram, WhatsApp and Uber is testimony to the rapid expansion of the brand when consumers take charge and brand managers become the enablers rather than owners of the brand. The brand in this situation has now truly come of age and brand managers can step back and mirror the mutual consumer conversations in their community.

Brand managers have to build very early in their brand development an avenue of social listening and consumer conversation. Today, technology is a great enabler to set multiple engagements but brands need to create opportunities and occasions for interactions. Brands that miss this opportunity severely short-change their growth potential.

Now, we get to the last part of cult brand, Mystique.

Mystique: If you take a celebrity or a revered person and understand him with his philosophy, achievements and all that he has done and spoken, you get a fairly good idea of the person, but it does not add up to the total personality of the person. Gandhi, Martin Luther King, Mandela can't be uncovered no matter how extensive the search into their person. The sum is just more than the total of the parts.

Cult brands are like that. They cannot be decomposed entirely by what they stand for and what they do. Something is still left out that defies logical exploring and sharing. It's a secret formula and cult brands retain a very small but very critical percentage of that inscrutable something or mystique which just cannot be explained.

How does one build mystique? Well, through doing all of the above and a few things even beyond the normal. People with mystique are just multi-faceted, exhibiting multiple talents and performances. Likewise, mystique in cult brands can come from many assets around a central identity as we explained before, but now we would add a lot of *rituals*. Not all of which are rational, but they add a lot to the brand's charm. Like the ritual of dunking an Oreo or opening a KitKat or the signature of Disney or the 'unboxing of iPhone'. These things say something but also leave a lingering something that builds stickiness and yearning amongst consumers that no amount of brand consumption satisfies. Mystique also comes from *elaborate imagery:*

the golden arches of McDonald's, the classic Coke calligraphy which is identifiable from miles away, the Star of Heineken, the swoosh of Nike—these fragments of brand identity are as powerful and as evocative as the full brand itself. *Music, smell, touch*—these are often underleveraged by brands but their ability to turn on the human mind and heart in multiple ways can hardly be doubted. Signature jingles of brands like Titan or Maggi, or perceived or real touch and the smell of paints (oil bound distemper of Dulux), cosmetics (feel of natural ingredients in Body Shop), fabrics (pashmina) of several brands are great secrets to build on. Finally, *nostalgia* is a great tool for cult brands to build mystique: the hostel waali Maggi, the first drink of Old Monk rum—can these stories ever be told with complete satisfaction? In fact, every time they are told, they leave a lot more unsaid for future stories as consumers supplement them with their intimate tales.

As you probe deeper, you can add more and more mystique elements with even legends and rumours that cult brands abound in, even if they are partially confirmed. So why does mystique work?

Brands are eventually about benefits, but everyone has their take on it. As brands get more elaborate, they speak to consumers individually in ways that cannot be aggregated. Mystique comes from the special chord that brands touch in every consumer's heart like a one-to-one friend even though they are universally available. This ineffable secret that a brand leaves in every single consumer's heart which is not shared with other users is a part of the mystique. Brands that miss building this personal intimacy don't have a special thing going for them with their lovers.

And cult brands are eventually signified by mad love for the brands.

Second-last Quarter

How Do I Surround My Consumer?

As we are stepping into the second half of the learning year, loaded with oodles of brand knowledge and experience of running the brand and managing oneself, it's time to look at the next pillar of development, which is building your team. This is also linked with the unique ability of the Shaper, in our STRIVES framework in chapter 1, who gives direction to the entire structure, process, people and technology of an assignment to ensure success. Of all the traits we discussed for a successful brand manager, Shaper has a seminal role in making you successful at work.

Managerial skill: shaper and specialist

Your team is not merely your direct reports but also those around you who contribute as peers, sometimes even seniors. What makes a Shaper tick and how can you acquire this quintessential trait of a leader?

Shapers show high adherence to the goal and vision of a team organized around a task. Their high result-orientation leads them to regard people, processes, technology and structure as stepping stones to the final objective. They see inter-connections, find synergies and weed out discordant pieces with ease. But unlike team workers who lay focus on joining people, they also excel at facilitating results. If people come in the way, as during cost-cutting exercises, they don't hesitate to take tough calls. Result takes precedence over all else.

How do you become a Shaper or enlist one for your cause? First, Shapers tend to be very *purposive* with an uncanny ability to spot or define the purpose of a team or a campaign. There is no activity without an end result for them. If there isn't a determinable output, they will abandon the task or force a conclusion out of an indeterminate situation. Second, Shapers are inveterate *optimizers*. The shortest route from one task to another in the most efficient way comes as naturally to them as innovating for Visionaries. Even before people can understand the landscape, they have already figured out the internal roads and alleys. Project managers can take their help to bring order to confusion and define expectations at all times. Third, they are *connectors* displaying an inherent tendency to connect elements of a project they have enlisted in a coherent whole. They make sub-teams, call review meetings, regroup mid-course if things are not working, enlist outside resources if required, and smoothen or eliminate friction when forces that delay project timelines crop up. Finally, they are blessed with a *mega-vision*. They see a project in its entirety from beginning to end with all indispensable pieces embedded nicely within. A perspective as comprehensive as this allows them to navigate the choppy waters with ease because when everyone's vision is blurred, they fly straight as the crow flies to the nest.

They seem to have all the traits of a leader who rallies resources to a cause but paradoxically, are just the opposite of a specialist not excelling in any field. Their span of work robs them of the ability to contribute to anything in detail. Their strength is not subject matter or innovation but an appreciation of the interconnections driven by a dogged resolve to realize the goal.

Specialist—the last managerial skill in our STRIVES framework—sees art in his profession. The job market may change, people may try to broad-base their skills and mistaken leaders may try to stretch them into new roles, but they adhere to their area of interest like a honeybee sticks to a beehive. They add to their domain of expertise vertically, upwards and downwards so intently day in and day out, that they become the most formidable professional in their field, almost unparalleled. Specialization can make them a god in a fortress, or leave them alone in the desert depending on whether the environment is favourable or not, but they are unlikely to change.

Think of that factory specialist, that financial analyst or the procurement guy who anticipates the commodities market with eerie certainty—you will be dead without these guys. They impart to business the fundamental trusses for growth and development. Without them, the functional aspect of brands would wither, making the brand irrelevant. As a brand manager, you would depend on the specialist in one area or the other because you are unlikely to have all the deep skills required in various areas of project management. Hence, it's critical to spot this talent and integrate it in your team for success.

Winning in markets everywhere

Now that we have covered the full brand development, it's time to deploy it to its full potential to reach consumers far and wide.

We discussed in the previous chapters that based on the analysis of sales volumes, market share, brand equity scores, penetration and lapsage data, we can determine what the consumer issue is, to tailor our brand response as outlined in chapter 5. We had therefore bucketed three issues which require the following responses:

Figure 10.1: Marketing solutions

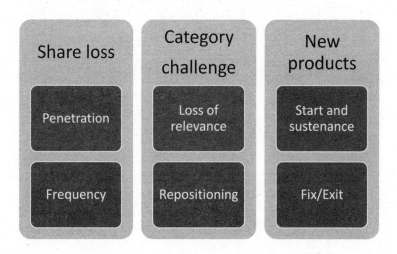

Let's try and look at some solutions for each of these six sub-issues based on our diagnostics. To link better with our NWB/BD pathway, it's important to highlight that the role of the brand is to assure consumers in the stage of want to convert into demand for itself. In each of these cases, the role of the brand differs. For instance:

- To increase penetration, it needs to expand its appeal to new consumers by explaining its reason to exist to consumers above competition's claims
- To increase frequency, the brand needs to appeal with either more uses, or more occasions to existing users
- To increase the category popularity, usually done by the market leader (though some followers can come in as disruptors and speak for the category to turn it in favour of itself, based on its benefits), the brand needs to remind consumers of its benefits
- To increase its popularity versus another category, for example, if fruit juices are gaining at the cost of carbonated beverages like

Pepsi or Coke, then these brands have to up their functional appeal and imagery to wean the consumers back
- Finally, if there is a lukewarm response to new products, then the answer lies in looking at various elements in marketing or even calling it quits if the situation is beyond redemption

In all the cases, the brand has to intervene, keeping its brand purpose in mind. Not doing so would amount to a knee-jerk reaction to the current problem which may be fixed today but cause erosion of core brand equity in the long term. Therefore, the intervention of the brand between want and demand with the right benefits and purpose is extremely critical, necessitating the steps mentioned in previous chapters on communication and brands.

To better understand each of these cases, we will take some examples from our experience across brands that we have had the opportunity to directly influence in various marketing leadership roles.

Share loss: Increasing penetration

Theme communication is referred to that fundamental piece of brand advertisement or copy which brings out the brand purpose and builds the brand's user base over time, explaining the brand's point of view. Let's deep-dive here into a power brand, Boost.

Boost is a choco-malt drink which was launched in 1976 to counter Bournvita. The brand made a landmark choice in the health drink space by signing up Kapil Dev with his characteristically rendered advertising tagline: 'Boost is the secret of my energy', which instantly struck recall and remembrance of brand benefits in the swashbuckling style of the all-rounder. The celebrity streak continued, keeping the brand ticking nicely with the evolving times. Sachin Tendulkar came on board in 1990 and stayed on for a record 25 years (the longest celebrity association we know of in India), catapulting the brand to an incontestable glory. Sehwag followed in 2002, M.S. Dhoni in 2008 and Virat Kohli in 2013. The changing communication copy and stars were strung together resolutely with the same tagline that Kapil launched (except Virat and Dhoni called it the secret of 'our' energy). There are not many brands with a consistency and singularity of approach like brand Boost.

While the reason to believe stayed the malt formula of Boost which imparted energy release, in 2009, the USP got more teeth with the claim '3X stamina' based on a successful clinical trial.

The Boost brand offers many learnings of strong brand management. What else did they do in the environment they played? While whites or the drinks like Horlicks were pivoted on nutrition, the brown drinks like Bournvita changed the narrative to power, energy and taste modification in keeping with the demand of the kids and teens who wanted better taste and a benefit of energy to get by for their energy-intense needs in the growing years. Boost got it right from the start by choosing sports as the metaphor of energy. It also imbued the brand with values of grit, determination, competitiveness and the desire to win which reflected positively in its brand personality. Deploying celebrities attracted eyeballs and brought a sense of aspiration and attitude to the brand. Other important brand tenets were consistent, like the rampant use of vibrant red in packaging and iconography.

If we now look at the communication framework, Boost worked on the fundamentals right. The need was for an energy-filled solution when the world was talking general nutrition. Then again, the gap or opportunity in the market was focusing on children with a specific offer for them, distinct from a general family nourisher that Horlicks was. Finally, the benefit that Boost was offering was energy which nailed the need with supreme satisfaction. What was the brand purpose that was sitting at the seminal juncture between want and demand to convince the consumers to buy Boost over Bournvita? After all, Boost had to gain share from the biggest player. The brand purpose of Boost has been steady throughout the entire journey:

'We exist to unleash the energy in you.'

It is clearly differentiated from other brands, speaks directly to the consuming audience and is based on the consumer insight that 'Kids are not afraid of competition and are willing to go all out to win'. In fact, winning gives them a high, but it's not easy and requires relentless hard work and energy to achieve. The brand archetype is clearly the conqueror or the winner who believes that you don't win silver, you lose gold. If you had to do a personality description of the archetype, you'd come up with: 'He is the boy or girl who has a busy schedule and needs lots of energy, is always up for challenges, wants to win and be seen as an ideal worth aspiring for just as he aspires to be like his cricket demi-gods Virat and Dhoni'. From this realistic portrayal, it became important that while the celebrity must be aspirational, he must not be distant, because he has to inspire kids to work harder and provide the expert opinion, energy and stamina for kids to achieve in their lives. In other words, demi-gods should be achievable.

For the above reason, the kid should be in active interaction with the celebrity, not an overwhelmed passive devotee who stays unaffected in real life by hero stories.

In spite of knowing the winning formula for Boost, things started to go a bit awry for Boost in the period 2009–11 with Horlicks (an internal competitor coming from the stable of GSK) and Bournvita chipping share. This also goes to indicate the importance of detailing communication elements to prevent going off-course. The copy in this period lost the kid connect, getting too focused on the clinical story of the stamina directed at the mothers, and due to low sports connect, and limited role of celeb and kid.

Learning from their mistakes, advertising in the period 2011–13 became focused on the kid and sports but unfortunately swung to the other extreme. The creatives in this period became gritty and dark, showing sweat and toil far in excess of a brand that kindled hope and performance in a natural encouraging, not punishing, way. The bright, livewire happy kid got pushed over by the grimly resolute kid which was out of character with the brand.

Imagery tests performed in 2014–15 showed that the brand showed a drop in kids' love and connect, and the promise of Boost was not exciting the kid any more. We did detailed diagnostics on the brand communication and its impact thereof and captured the following gaps and opportunities:

- Kellogg's Chocos and Bournvita had upped the kid appeal quotient with better flavours and more relatable communication. The world of Boost was instead being seen as adult with loads of seriousness
- The world of Boost had to be bright, optimistic and cheerful, not grim and intense
- Celebrities had to be guides and mentors not hogging the limelight leaving the kid in oblivion. Instead, an active kid waiting to be a hero was the desired world from the point of view of the consumers
- Instead of showing alienating science, there was a need to shift to semiotics, visuals and language that were more pro-children

With the following learnings, a detailed insight generation programme was run which yielded following insights:

- The child believes that he can be omnipotent, all powerful with no place for weakness
- He or she doesn't believe in neck-to-neck competition, but he wants unchallenged victory, a complete rout
- He or she wants to be a saviour, someone others can always fall back on
- Winning amongst peers is no big deal. Taking on tougher, bigger opponents is the real deal

From the above, the last insight was selected as the winning consumer insight after in-depth discussion and groups with kids and moms. From this opportunity came the brand purpose of enabling kids to take on bigger challenges and this led to the big idea:

'Boost's energy helps me play the bigger game.'

Based on this insight, the creative brief was detailed to include a story that the kids could relate to but equally matched with an audacious aspiration capturing the higher brand purpose this time around with bold visuals and arresting metaphors. From this was born the creative depicting a doughty kid who takes on Virat and surprises him with his winning strokes with bright, vibrant imagery without the grim intensity of before.

Following the campaign, market share started to swing upwardly. The value share of the brand moved by 190 bps from 26.8 to 28.7 in the period 2016–19, and volume share from 30.7 to 34.7 in the same period, with all the Southern states responding. The penetration of the brand also moved up from 23.7 per cent to 30.9 per cent in the same period. The brand scores moved up as Boost became the preferred brand from another choice in the morning repertoire.

Share loss, increasing frequency through micro-marketing

The opportunity to recover market share needn't come only from reversing lapsage or increasing penetration, but also from increasing frequency of consumption amongst the same consumers. The campaign was supplemented with a strong digital engagement with the target audience called the 'Boostcamp' where today's potential stars would train to become tomorrow's champions through a detailed step-by-step training using digital technology that deployed 'stamina and training' as the clear points of difference for the brand.

Through this campaign, Virat and Dhoni demonstrated exclusively for Boost consumers difficult shots and stumping techniques while having their Boost to supplement their energy. More importantly, this was multiplied by association with the World Cup happening at the same time through kids getting tips on stamina and training for winning behind the scenes. The result was that, without being an official sponsor of the World Cup, Boost became associated with the World Cup hype, driving the brand's topicality, appeal and eventually consumption as the World Cup saga unfolded in every Indian household in the run-up to the event as well as during, creating many occasions for consumption and increasing the frequency of consumption by 10–15 per cent in different Southern states where this event was hosted.

Integrated marketing, which stands for well-pieced elements of marketing across various touchpoints, was activated with many other supporting initiatives run with active partnership with sales (including similar rewards on strength and stamina for the winning territories) such as:

- Association with sports leagues in the various states such as ISL (Indian Super League) and PBL (Premium Badminton League)
- Programmes held in sub-district and rural India at the grassroots level advocating sports and stamina, tied up with the Boostcamp campaign that became a stellar example of how the brand purpose was being brought alive on the ground
- Strong visibility was activated on ground in traditional and modern trade with eye-catching POS and shelf-ready display packs to drive accessibility

However, big brands like Boost and Horlicks require *micro-marketing* to maximize the impact on ground. For this, a detailed analysis was undertaken per political state, cross-tabbed with the state of the consumer's attitude towards the brand and category, and town class based on population to arrive at the best marketing solution as we had seen in the chapter on targeting. A similar study can be undertaken for your brand and the result collated to arrive at a micro-marketing grid as below:

Figure 10.2: Micro-marketing by region

State	Town class	Targeted consumer	Opportunity	Action	Metric
Core market: TN and Kerala	< 5 lakh	ANT (aware not tried) and lapsers	Drive relevance of stamina	Large packs	Distribution increase, volume offtake
Opportunity market: AP, Karnataka	Across all towns in urban, rural by selection	Urban and rural ANT/ lapsers	Driving relevance for stamina (urban)/ Driving awareness of value for money (rural)	Large pack (urban), small pack placement drive (rural)	Vol. offtake, numeric distribution of small pack
Expansion market: West Bengal	Urban	Non-HFD users	Drive trials for the pack basis value and relevance of energy and stamina	Small pack, sachet drive	Numeric, Per Dealer Offtake (PDO)
Expansion market: Maharashtra	Urban, semi-urban	SEC A/B/C users of Bournvita	Relevance of stamina	Small pack, large pack in big towns	Numeric distribution, vol. offtake, market share

Given the differential nature of the task, there were plenty of regional adaptations apart from the main theme creative: film on small pack, and Boostcamp and short duration films on the value of small packs. Media was chosen based on the need from TV to local regional channels to digital in metros and non-metros in Maharashtra. Thus, the erstwhile single-stroke approach was replaced by micro-marketing.

As a result of the theme campaign and the multiplier on the ground, the average consumption measured in kg per household moved from 1.38 to 1.47 kg in the period 2016–19 for the above geographies.

Another example of firing up consumption of the category is the launch of chilled Horlicks to increase consumption during the summers when sales typically take a dip with kids preferring cold beverages. Launched with 'Kuch bhi karega' for Horlicks campaign, including a YouTube channel with the same name, it invited kids to participate in fun challenges during the summer like: No mobile for a day, finish your tiffin, attend all the lab classes. *Integrated marketing* or the term used to describe 360-degree amplification of a campaign across different media touchpoints was kicked off by content integration in popular toon shows like *Chhota Bheem*, gamification to engage kids in digital with product integration and rewards and sharing focused on chocolate Horlicks.

Extensive sampling, recipes on social media and search engines, and strategic partnerships with various beverage-vending parlours were taken to extend the salience. To assure consumers about the superiority of the product, various taste challenges were conducted on ground too. User-generated content (UGC) on recipes was encouraged to multiply consumer engagement and rewards were given on multiple purchases to create a loyalty loop. Finally, to extend reach and get many more trials, a trial pack at an accessible Rs 30 price point was launched. Finally, to fire off kids pester-power, a promotion of a fancy bottle and collectible cards came into play to strengthen relationships with kids. Below is the whole integrated marketing campaign that made this a huge success.

Figure 10.3: Integrated marketing for chilled Horlicks

The results were an increase of 230 bps in market share within the quarter, and 80 bps increase in one year. Launch of the trial pack increased the outlet base to one million outlets rapidly.

Category challenge: lack of relevance

Category erosion is a serious task. Often the threat coming from outside the category is not perceived till much later and when the diagnosis is apparent, redeeming actions are neither obvious nor easy. It requires looking outside the category to take on unknown challengers, compared to market share wars against brands that behave similarly in the same category. However, timely action can not only save the category but also give disproportionate gains since the brand gets added benefits of proximal categories, which would not have been possible in the normal course of business, enhancing overall consumption.

In HFD, our experience has been that if you don't build the category at opportune moments, you could lose out on recruiting new consumers. From our previous sales trends, we understood qualitatively that during exam times in the Indian academic calendar, if the brand is not active, it loses out. Conversely, if it's active and in conversation with relevant news, it can actually turn out to be a goldmine for increasing penetration.

Led by this knowledge, we designed the highly successful 'Horlicks exam time' campaign as a supplement to the main 'Badhne ki bhookh' campaign which has been discussed in the previous chapter on communication.

During exam time, children are stressed and the nutrition needs are the highest. Looking at this deprivation, Horlicks being the great nourisher found a unique opportunity to step in and make a difference in keeping with its brand purpose by:

- Preparation: Turning the boring planning and preparation to inspiring planning and preparation
- Emotional nutrition: from policing nutrition by the mothers in this period to becoming an emotional support

If you thus infuse the new kind of preparation and emotional nutrition, the brand stands to provide a 'fearless exam' experience in the most critical ninety days of the kid's life, every year.

Based on this idea, a fresh TV film was created and a huge ground engagement plan was made based on students coaching for IIT in the city of Kota, which won critical acclaim and viralled instantly across India. Mothers of students appearing for exams were taken by the brand to visit their unexpecting students in the middle of their hectic exam preparation. Their spontaneous reaction and joy on seeing their parents, and getting showered by their love at the most critical juncture of their life, was captured and played for many parents and students who vicariously identified with it.

The brand purpose of being the emotional support was amply brought out, getting immense positive mileage for Horlicks. This was followed with more of such parents visiting or sending their greetings with a 'box of love' including Horlicks to their kids in Hyderabad delivered by a tie-up with the railways, and soon the idea became a rage in India winning many Cannes and Abby awards. The 'Fearless Kota' campaign reached, through a mix of organic and inorganic campaigns, as many as 82 million people on YouTube and 26 million on Facebook, achieving monstrous popularity.

Micro-marketing was followed for the exam time with many multipliers: songs were played by A.R. Rahman and local stars in different regions belittling exam fear as portrayed in the Bengali rendition '*Bhoy khabo na, Horlicks khabo* (Don't eat hunger, eat Horlicks)'. Fearless songs as they came to be called were played on the radio by famous RJs; Rob was roped in to multiply the kid appeal on the *M.A.D.* programme on Pogo and even integrations in TV programmes was undertaken to contextualize the brand in consumers' lives. Positive PR was generated when the scourge of exams as a source of depression and anxiety was taken on and experts were roped in to counsel students. Banners and streamers were put up in retail stores explaining how Horlicks improves concentration and attention, which was clinically proven.

Category challenge: repositioning

A more serious threat to the category arises when its relevance comes into question. This happened to the dairy whitener category which is used extensively in the east and the south to make tea, since liquid milk was historically scarce in these geographies. However, with the white revolution, better logistics and introduction of tetrapacks that allowed milk to be either transported or stored longer, the format of powder on account of its 'un-naturality' (compared to the original version of the liquid milk) fell out of favour with consumers. Over three years, from 2013–16, the category saw an erosion of nearly 8–10 per cent amongst major brands Amulya and Whitemagic, while a slew of local brands were virtually wiped out.

Here was an existential threat and the market leaders did deep consumer insighting, going through the cycle of understanding the deprivation for the consumers and finding gaps or tension to convert a non-existent want for their product into a demand of powder over liquid.

Following this, they reacted with communication based on the intrinsic goodness of powder and re-positioned the dairy powder as the superior cup based on: consistent end-cup delivery (the quality of liquid milk in the markets was still not that good), thicker mouthfeel (the fat in powder is saved in the powder format and reconstitutes to deliver a coat of fat that consumers like, unlike milk which loses fat over successive boiling as the layer of cream we see when milk boils), ease of storage and preparation, and even better value for money considering all of these factors.

Consumers who were long used to the powder walked back into the category, arresting some of the decline and today, nearly half the households are getting used to double usage of both powder and milk, finding a use for each format. Timely communication and reinstatement of the old benefits saved the category from extinction and now the brands of this category face the task of upgrading value constantly for the consumer since liquid milk is bound to improve, threatening the powder format which is seen to be more regressive by consumers.

Another example of eroding category relevance is the category of disposable contact lenses that seemed to suddenly stagnate after a good start. The old solution of glasses was making a comeback as marketers rushed to consumers finding reasons for lapsage and relaunched the product with renewed focus. Lenses were hence repositioned as the 'hassle-free choice of the new confident generation'. Eye check-up camps were organized and people were made aware of their weak eyesight and initiated straight into the contact lens category, thereby broadening the base of users. Also, youngsters wearing spectacles were encouraged to take to lenses to look better and be at ease while indulging in sports, before they would get resigned to the use of spectacles.

Later, a host of coloured, disposable and easy-to-use lenses with low maintenance were launched to wean consumers into the category based on what appealed or ailed them—a conclusion of a detailed segmentation study done. The result was a reversal of the decline and the start of an upswing that continues to move up today with a steady irreversible cumulative annual growth.

Marketing rooted in systematic consumer understanding can thus come to the rescue to steady a category on the verge of extinction (dairy whitener) or revive another that is challenged by an older category of spectacles that consumers keep lapsing back to due to long usage (lenses).

New products

New products are a tricky animal (more in the chapter on innovation next) since their journey is never a linear upward trend. They are marked by a strong start, weak start, slow follow-up, sudden increase or no reaction at all. The irony is that an erratic journey of this kind can happen in spite of positive research preceding the launch, well-aligned company or financial support, or even consistent tracking and monitoring. Whatever the situation, consumer listening and placing corrective actions are the only solutions out of this quicksand of ill-fated investment of time and resources.

We will take a few examples of new products with different journeys to understand the criticality of following the basics of understanding need, segmentation and positioning as discussed in the previous chapters.

Great start, acceleration subsequently: Lehar Kurkure of Frito-Lay India was a success from the word go. The product format based on the fusion of the appeal of the taste of traditional Indian snacks with the finger-picking ease of western snacks (unlike the messy palmful of Indian namkeens) delighted users across age and socio-economic segments. For nearly a year, the product sold on just product placement and trials generated from retail visibility. But with consumer feedback on the wide acceptability of the product, a marketing campaign was launched under the umbrella brand Lehar called 'Kya karein, control nahi hota' (what to do, can't control). The brand grew by leaps and bounds and has subsequently seen iconic campaigns like 'Meetha sheetha chodo, Kurkure lo', undertaking an anti-positioning against the sweet snacking especially during festive seasons to the current 'Tedha hai, par mera hai' (it's crooked, but still it's mine) which depicts its physical format and the unpredictable fun inhered in it.

Great start, sustained continuously: Sensodyne, a niche product with an explosive performance, had a promising start giving the consumers an opportunity to once again enjoy their cold, sour and hot food after being impacted by tooth sensitivity and losing all hope of enjoying their food normally. It made the right moves focusing on the rampant tooth sensitivity built convincingly through one- to-one dentist endorsement, followed by mass media education of ailing consumers. Clear deprivation understanding, converting the latent want into a demand with explicit benefits and cueing the happy world subsequent to product usage—ticks all fronts of marketing discussed in previous chapters.

Slow start, gradual pick-up: Women's Horlicks made a lot of sense at the time of launch. For a significant section of Horlicks consumers, a solution made specifically for women's needs and positioned on the all-round benefits coming from calcium, iron and the whole ensemble of nutrients. But it didn't quite take off the way it was expected. Consumer response was a trickle even as investment and efforts were going north. What could be done?

Consumer research revealed the need for highlighting a sharp deprivation and bringing about a tension or a gap that necessitated urgent action. Enlightened with this reality, the brand team chose to create a story focusing on one of the many problems (villain) facing women: osteopenia and osteoporosis—the rampant debilitating problems of depleting bone density, the imminent onset of which could be checked by building a bone-bank if corrective steps were taken.

And hence, Women's Horlicks was repositioned as the solution for building bones based on the goodness of easily absorbed calcium which would stall, even prevent, the horrible disability waiting for women down the ageing road. The sharper repositioning (vindicating the rule of singularity, referred to earlier) brought energy to the lukewarm response and now Women's Horlicks is continuously increasing penetration, becoming a relevant solution to the women who need to look after themselves when they are finished with the family.

Slow start, and burial: If marketing supports solutions then it also champions the exit of a lost cause if the proposition is not attractive.

We have seen in earlier chapters the cases where you either fix or exit. There are times when no amount of investment yields the desired result, leaving no choice but to quit and redeploy energies elsewhere. The industry is full of examples of withdrawals, but timely ones done with business acuity, saving expenses and giving inspiration for future launches, are few and far between.

Nano took a long time getting called off the shelves even though its positioning of being the dream of two-wheeler owners came a cropper (by making the car look very wannabe in the eyes of other car owners) very early. The company that launched Thums Up, Parle Agro, tried their hand more recently with a unique coffee blend called Café Cuba. It was a carbonated coffee beverage that fused Parle's expertise in fizzy drinks with the emerging trend of cold coffee consumption that was touted to be the next disruption in beverages. However it was a disaster because the codes of 'stimulating aroma of roasted beans', its stated unique proposition, did not quite click with consumers who were expecting the creamy, milk taste of coffee and found the fizz at odds with the experience of a known cold dairy beverage. The brand failed to make any impact in retail shelves. The winning team of yesteryear learnt their lesson but their learning is still to see the next success taking birth. Horlicks Foodles that was meant to be the healthy counter to noodles from the stable of healthy and trusted Horlicks sank without a trace, lacking a differentiated idea or a credible counter positioning. Amul's repeated foray into chocolates with questionable success repeatedly proves that a strong brand cannot just entail successful sub-variants without understanding and dominating category rules.

New products therefore present challenges of various hues and we will explore more of this in the subsequent chapters as we unravel the last aspect of marketing, delving into the product.

Final Quarter

Where, Why, When Do I Innovate?

Office art: Building a team

As we get to the end of our brand mastership in the same breath as we learn to manage the office, we need to add the managerial skill of building a team around us. Brand management sits at the intersection of many roads and team co-ordination below and around has a direct bearing on the success of your endeavours. As you become senior, you will manage a clutch of brands, leading a team of diverse skills. You need to be cognizant of the skills required for managing teams, eventually growing them around you to support your cause of growing the brand (not to become an adept politician, be forewarned of the critical difference in the objective).

For that you need to analyse your team's potential. You will always get a mixed bag of self-starters, laggards, push-overs and those who need to be driven as against those who need to be booted out. Spotting them early and using their skills and motivations is critical to project success. Develop a way to judge people based on their competence or how well they know their job, their ability to deploy it with good judgement on the job, the energy they bring to bear on the assignment, the focus with which they pursue it and the relationships they are able to forge, building trust amongst co-workers and eventually with you. While checking them, design projects that objectively get you an answer to the above questions but don't be closed to verbal and non-verbal cues at the same time. How they react to opposition, how doggedly they pursue their goals, what methods do they deploy to get work done or shirk it—all these need to be visible to you without too much effort.

Once you have a mental map of their capabilities, make a plan to retain and grow those who are indispensable, manage the ones who matter but don't have long-term prospects, move the square pegs in round holes, and replace the trouble-makers who are not pulling their weight. You need to move with speed but apply brakes where required to not derail ongoing work. At all times, display respect and firmness to indicate professionalism with sensitivity as others try to assess your leadership style.

As the team starts to take shape, spell out the vision of the brand, avoid criticizing failures of the past to distract energy and build a positive conversation towards making a positive change. Let brand growth, consumer respect and trust, and individual growth for all be the fuel for growth, sidestepping all critical conversation of others. This will not only keep your focus and your teams in the right direction but also eliminate office grapevine and malicious conversations from eating into your work effectiveness, which you will have little time to attend to. Remember brand growth is what committed marketers live and die by. There is no alternative.

Finally, put milestones, fix mid-course reviews, make amends, and celebrate successes, point out failures (chide if the intention to succeed is lacking) in learning and keep growing this virtuous circle with sincere adherence to timelines and goals. Even though the vision is set by you, make sure you build consensus from below whenever required, or consult and advise as the situation may warrant, but increase participation in decision making to make results a collaborative output.

When do you know your team is working fine? When you step out of the office and nothing changes behind your back. Better still, when you discover one day that they have more energy than you infused them with. At that point, you can sit back and plan your next big move.

Now, over to the last brand competence that you will sharpen in your last three months of brand mastership: Innovation.

Innovation paradigm

Innovations are required constantly to upgrade a portfolio with consumer demands. Yet in spite of the best efforts of marketers, most innovations fail. Less than 5 per cent products survive after three years of launch and in some places in the world, the success rate could be as low as 2 per cent. Innovations are an elusive entity. You are disappointed if you do, and doomed if you don't. In spite of this bleak reality, you have no choice but to keep trying and even though it takes a lot of marketers' time, it doesn't always yield the desired results on their business. So how do we maximize the chances of success?

Most companies follow some standardized tools and templates for innovating routinely. Most have the following common steps:

- Ideation
- Concept creation
- Prototyping
- Testing
- Industrialization and commercialization

We will look at each of these stages and also delve into what measures to follow post launch, to minimize failures.

Ideation

Consumers don't show up at your door asking for innovation; in fact, they don't so much as rustle any discontent with your product lines to even trigger innovation. Marketers have to keep looking routinely or erratically for ways to service consumer needs better at all times. The more rigorously it's done, the stronger the chance that your brand outstrips others in spotting an innovation opportunity that will fulfil consumers' needs.

Ideation creates worthwhile direction for new opportunities when it's an intersection between consumer insight, product attributes and the benefits to be offered to consumers. Consumer insight generates the deprivations with current offerings in the consumer's need-states. Product attributes detail the variables on which the current offering can be improvised, and benefit is the resultant output that will come from revisiting consumer insight and product features. This will be clear as we dive further into each of these segments.

Figure 11.1: Ideation intersection

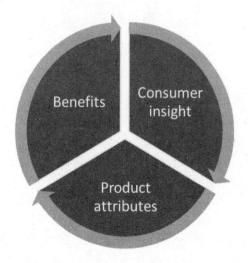

Consumer insight has been explained in the previous chapters in the context of research and communication. The process is the same; however, we are seeking solutions at the level of products or services to better service consumer needs. Consumer insight is meaningful when it evolves by toggling between consumer need, category and cultural codes. This needs to be understood as a process before we look at concrete examples.

Figure 11.2: Consumer insight

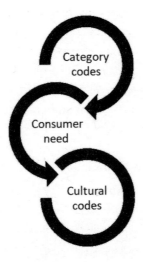

We have discussed about *consumer need* at length earlier. The beginning of the insighting process is understanding from discussions with consumers (in-depth one-to-one to focus group or even structured questionnaires) their state of satisfaction of their needs.

Understanding consumers' hidden desires and barriers will also require a robust understanding of the *cultural codes*. Ethnographic studies are useful to mine the latent cultural and social underpinnings shaping the consumers' values and beliefs. For instance, while consumers may talk about wanting quick breakfast solutions as their pressing need in the early morning rush, they are not willing to accept cold cereals. A mother's active and caring intervention, an absolute must in Indian households, is upheld when the food is hot. Further mining of the code of hot food revealed that hot stands for fresh. Therefore, cold cereal is neither fresh, nor from mother's hands, making it an absolute no-no for the pristine breakfast occasion which is her last control on child nutrition before they leave for school for the day.

Sometimes, consumers' values and beliefs are rooted in the history and mythology of the country and brand stories that inadvertently run counter to this stand the risk of outright rejection, which marketers may not able to fathom easily. Advertisements which show mothers as tough taskmasters, willing to step back to let the child be on her own, may work in the West but in India, it runs counter to the ideal of motherhood. This is built on the archetype of indulgent Yashoda's *laalan-poshan* (a unique Indian word that cues the loving-nourishing style of parenting) of Krishna, which mothers see themselves as a shadow of, becoming a happy heir to the rich cultural history of India. Ethnography studies reveal such cultural watch-outs that ought to be not transgressed without care.

Category codes bring to light the sum of all offerings by your brand and competitors that define the consumer experience in the category. Since no brand plays in all the spaces, it's instructive to know how the consumer experience has been in other need-states of competition to avoid being a me-too, worse still making the same mistake as others.

If you are working on Sprite, as an example, you must know what colas, orange drinks, cloudy lemon drinks, juices, even milk drinks are offering to understand what opportunities are being optimally satisfied or not by your competition. This allows you to embrace what's working and only choose what can potentially work. In this regard, it's useful to define the category wider than the narrowest definition. Thus, in the example above, we aren't looking merely at carbonated beverages but also juices and milk drinks to appreciate what consumers could be toying with. As will be explained later, a view of proximal categories opens avenues for newer innovation.

Intersecting these three, therefore, one gets the consumer insight. With that framework and using secondary research, market immersions and expert interviews, we created the following examples for a) HFD category, b) Cold beverages, and c) Chips. As you plough through the insights, you would notice they are gleaned with a view to capture the current experience and also indicate dissatisfaction to lead to new opportunities. In that sense, insights almost appear like wish statements. If insights don't capture the desire of consumers for a better, alternative experience, they usually become non-actionable. Below are statements that lead to consumer insight, captured succinctly in italics.

- 'Too many ready to eat foods are taking away my ability to influence what goes into the food and compromises my role as the nourisher of the family': *Mother's touch*
- 'I distrust packaged foods from the way they look and feel. I wish I could have the comfort of choosing natural, everyday fruits and vegetables in these new-age foods': *Natural food*
- 'Even though my kids want it and other mothers are falling for it, I don't know what's in the packaged food. When I read the ingredients, my discomfort only goes up': *Clean labelling*
- 'I understand that nutrition is important but all-round health requires other things also: exercise, sleep, sports, mental activities. How do I complement my food with these things to see a distinct difference in my kids in today's competitive world?': *Holistic solutions*
- 'We grew up having health drinks but these days they only communicate to kids. Is Horlicks not the drink for us any more? It seems like we are going on because of old habits': *Age-specific offer*

- 'I am pulled apart between what my mother-in-law tells me and the digital posts and forwards. Deluged by excessive information, I don't know what's good for me, what should I act on, what should I discard': *Information need*

Some more insights from the cold beverages category, in a similar way:

- 'The taste of cola is incomparable but it's unhealthy with high sugar content that makes it almost addictive': *Healthy cola*
- 'I believed that juices were healthier than aerated beverages till I read the sugar label. They seem to be as bad. Now I distrust all packaged drinks': *Low sugar packaged drinks*
- 'Dairy-based drinks are a great alternative, but they are so heavy and appear so dated that kids just don't seem to take to it like they take to soft drinks': *Dairy modernized*

And, from the chips category, which is led by Lay's:

- 'Chips are great fun, but I wish the packs also came with sauces like salsa, imli—it would double the delight': *Chip-n-dip*
- 'Potato chips have been traditionally available in local namkeen shops, but other chips made from banana, corn, tapioca offer a good change once in a while, but the local options of these aren't good enough': *Alternative chips*
- 'The crunch of chips is irresistible, but their fried profile makes them very unhealthy and I refrain from indulging myself': *Fit chips*

As can be seen from the above examples, the consumer insight has been constructed using a) need satisfaction state with the brand and categories, b) cultural codes about the role of mother, trust in traditional ingredients has been uncovered, and c) category codes pertaining to the generic or non-specific nature of the offerings of all have been captured. This gives a set of insights which can be further chiselled to reach specific product and service pillars.

With the knowledge of the consumer's ask, it's time to get into the product code to understand our limitations. It's important to understand that for innovating we have to look far and also within. If we only see consumer insight and disregard product boundaries, we may come up with solutions that are too wild to be implemented for our needs. Likewise, if we stay within the ambit of product definition, we are unlikely to bring something fresh and valuable to the market. Hence, consumer insight has to be supplemented with meaningful product attributes to innovate in a radical way.

Product attributes

Any brand has certain variables specific to the product class it belongs to. In the next step, we unravel this at the middle of the innovation process so we can look at consumer insight on one side and new benefits on the other side, keeping product attributes as the centre of change.

At this stage, we detail the product features that are currently in consideration by consumers. However, for this exercise, we look not at the specifics of experience but the variables underneath. As an example, if you are working on brand Pepsi, your consumer is experiencing the brand across these variables: taste, fizz, temperature, thickness of beverage, colour, aroma, bubbling sound of soda, tactile feel of the bottle (its shape, the dew drops of cold storage), the satiety or belly feel and the throat experience after drinking.

Looking at these variables, one can explore alternatives and arrive at fresh benefits for ideation. Before we detail that, let's understand the last piece in ideation: Benefits.

Benefits

Benefits for consumers are of three kinds:

- *Incremental:* The existing product with a minor tweak gives consumers an additional reason to consume; however, long-term continuation of sales with this route cannot be assured. This serves more to generate excitement and occasionally even increase the base of users. Innovations like flavours, new style and designs, new features qualify for this bucket of innovation.
- *Expansive:* Deeper, more elaborate innovations that alter product format, features and experience substantially so that while some semblance with the original is retained, the experience of the new is enhanced over the old. Chips with dips, Bournvita taste in biscuit format, tubeless tyres, fixed deposits with facilities of liquid investment—these innovations expand the consumer's interaction with the product by bringing benefits of some other categories often, or extending brands into new categories altogether.
- *Disruptive:* Here the benefits are completely unexpected, taking the consumer by surprise and creating unimagined brand interactions. Such benefits can be a game changer with segmentation revisited. Mobile phones over landline, hand sanitizers over soaps, phone cameras in place of old cameras. All these have reconfigured the old categories, setting up new expectations and deliveries.

Now that we have the consumer insight, the understanding of current product attributes and the various levels of benefits that we can offer to consumers, it's time to churn out innovation ideas. Let's generate three ideas from each category above fusing insights with product codes and benefits.

1. HFD: Age-specific offer (consumer insight) of Horlicks for kids, adults, women catering to their specific nutrition with

taste, texture, bite (product attributes), offering different tastes (incremental benefit), in snack bars (expansive benefit) or even Horlicks family nutrition advisory service (disruptive benefit).

2. Cold beverage: Modernized dairy (consumer insight) for teens and young adults offering differentiated taste, freshness, satiety (product attributes) in cool plastic bottles or cans or single-serve options (incremental benefit), available in school and colleges, even through vending machines (expansive benefit), and dairy bites and bars giving the goodness of milk and proteins in dry, easy-to-carry formats (disruptive benefits).

3. Chips: Fit chips for health freaks (consumer insight) with taste as good as conventional chips (product attribute), available in unsalted but spiced up flavours (incremental benefit), in crunchy forms other than saddle shape of natural chips (expansive benefit), made in age-appropriate calorific portions and forms to take the edge off hunger and not disturb the appetite for the main meal (disruptive benefit).

Above are some illustrative examples of firing off your ideation process in a way that you touch the skies without losing your feet in the category you play in. This way, it's in keeping with your firm's competence or brand's purpose and still allows it to foray into new areas to capitalize on emerging opportunities. Below is a grid with some more examples to tickle your grey cells before we deep-dive into concept writing, the next stage in innovation.

Figure 11.5: Ideation cross table

Category	Consumer insight	Product attributes	Incremental benefit	Expansive benefit	Disruptive benefit
HFD	Mother's touch	Total solution	Communication focusing on mother's touch, mother moments with kids	Recipes that requires mother's intervention	Products that are designed such that mothers add products from their kitchen to complete it.
	Natural food	Malt, sugar, cocoa	Packaging gives sourcing details	Organic ingredients	Special formula with traditional Indian grains known for their Ayurvedic benefits
	Information need	Detailed food chart, vitamin pre-mix benefits	Simplified nutrition charts detailing benefits with growth parameters	Website as service pillar to guide consumers through nutrition needs	Horlicks nutrition counselling, Horlicks nutrition academies with leading hospitals
Chips	Chip-n-dip	Ingredients	Sachets of salsa, tamarind chutneys	Chip-n-dip recipes and party ideas	Chip meals in partnership with restaurants and Swiggy, Zomato
	Alternative chips	Potatoes, edible oil, salt, crunchy bite, salt and seasoning	Tapioca, corn, yam chips	Food in the shape of chips	Crunchy bites with unconventional shapes, sizes available
Cold beverages	Healthy cola	Sugar, concentrate, black colour, fizz	Low sugar, diet or zero cola with aspartame	Grape, mango, strawberry flavours with aeration	Cola appearance vitamin water
	Low sugar packaged drinks	Sugar, concentrates, fizz	Reduced portion size, light sugar (60 per cent) with new flavours to mask low sugariness	Low sugar complex flavours (that have no benchmark taste) in packs that resemble home tumblers and cups	Do it yourself kit to make at home with low sugar concentrate

As can be seen from the above, innovations are not restricted to products alone. Even communication and consumer engagement ideas can emerge from this detailed exercise.

So, we have got some ideas here but how innovative are they? We can be more outrageous in our ideas, or we can do less and become predictable. How do we decide that we are not going too far out of the brand's reach and we are also not being very conservative? This question can be handled if we do a 'brand stretch' study wherein we examine the core attributes of a brand that are absolutely integral to the brand, without which the brand would not be able to hold. For instance, Eno antacid stands for the trademark fizz (generated when the powder dissolves in water, almost symbolic of what happens in the consumer's ailing stomach), speed and gentleness. If these core values are retained in the new ideas, the brand can take the stretch; if not, the new idea will not hold and marketers may have to evaluate a new brand. For a brand stretch study to work, it's important, therefore, to know the core brand attributes that are known by consumers as also those that have been built by marketers deliberately.

Concept: After writing the idea and having a few options (at this stage we have many ideas since we are not sure how many will eventually meet the consumers' approval), we have to write the concept to represent the ideas as best as the intention and gauge consumers' response.

Writing a concept is tricky. It has to be just right. If you overpromise, disappointment with the actual product is certain. On the contrary, if you underwhelm the consumer with lukewarm communication, then they may never show up at your door and you will kill a good idea prematurely. How does one pitch the idea to the consumer, therefore, just as it is? Since this is a stage at which a go, no-go decision is reached for ideas, it's important that we screen concepts very cautiously. So, how do we create a concept?

A good concept has the following elements, all of which must be adhered to with rigour to ensure a comprehensive exposure. The elements of a good concept are:

- *Innovation name*: The innovation idea should be clearly brought out in the fewest words describing the consumer offer as best as possible. It should have a hint of ingredient, a hint of functionality or a benefit, so the idea grabs consumers and sets them up with a basic expectation. Sometimes a qualifier below a crisp main title also helps. For instance, 'Horlicks health sticks—a healthy whole grain delicious snack for busy kids'.
- *When you need it*: gives the reason for this innovation. The occasion or the mental state when the need of this innovation is felt.
- *What is it*: If you have the consumer hooked from above, you need to tell them transparently what the product is in order that their curiosity is addressed immediately? Special features which set this innovation apart should be called out since this is when the consumer is most attentive if the previous two steps are well executed.
- *What it does*: Elaborate the benefit that consumers will unequivocally enjoy.
- *How does it do it*: Establish functionally the reason why it will deliver the benefit, leaving no scope for not believing it.
- *Lastly, reiterate the benefit*: Before leaving the consumer, re-emphasize the benefit so that if the consumer is sitting on the fence, he is lured over to your proposition.

Based on the structure above, here is an example of a concept card:

Horlicks Multigrain-Health Sticks

Health in tasty, any time bites

Want taste and health with the convenience of junk food any time, when children ask but can't find it?

Presenting Horlicks Multigrain Health Sticks that come with the goodness of five grains, packed with energy, vitamins and milk proteins. It offers a quick and wholesome bite for the frequent hunger pangs of your kids.

Filled with essential fibre and taste, your kids will finally have the energy to keep chasing their dreams.

Available in four flavours, suitable for tiffins or snack boxes, hunger will never be a concern now.

In the above concept card, it helps if the drawing of the prototype is shown along with the price to give consumers a clear picture of what to expect.

So, you have screened many concepts and based on the response, you have two or three winning ideas. Next comes the stage of prototyping.

Prototype: From the shortlisted ideas, it's good to make some prototypes and do a concept-product research. Here, half the testing audience (typically focus groups) gets the product first and the other half gets the concept first—to eliminate the first placed bias. Then, consumer reaction is taken on the likeability of both the concept and the product, one after another with specific asks that you want to emphasize along with purchase intention and mention of price. Three scenarios are possible from the study:

- Concept scores higher than the product: In this case, the product needs to be improvised or the concept toned down to avoid disappointment when consumers try the product.
- Product scores higher than the concept: Rewrite the concept basis consumer feedback capturing what consumers have liked about the product.
- Concept and product are evenly matched and likeability is high: This is the winning proposition that is ready to go into the next state of industrial trial and commercial launch.

Industrial trial, Commercial launch

From the prototype which is usually taken by the research and development team on the final manufacturing set-up or a similar one, product manufacturing is planned. Final P&L, ingredient closure with vendors, packaging options and assumptions on variable manufacturing costs are frozen so the product is finally getting ready. It's important to sync the minimum order quantity (MOQ) with your selling ability. Just the right amount needs to be made or even slightly less than what the market can demand to create an initial suction on the stocks that generates positive sentiments and gives the launch a head start. If the MOQ is high, it's advisable to make a lower quantity at a higher cost, test market the product and only then proceed to launch totally to avoid writing off new products initially.

This is important because many good products are deemed to be failures based on the supply and demand imbalance. When in fact, consumers like it and can have more if the whole supply chain servicing their demand is fine-tuned.

Failures are judged based on the first few weeks of the product's performance. This is a fatal flaw. Apart from the supply-demand imbalance being misread, there are other corrections that can be made to ensure success for a project that was conceived for a long time but executed in a very short time and summarily dismissed for the wrong reasons. From our experience, we have found the following errors in innovations that need to be watched out for after launch.

Isolate success reasons from failures: Success is never complete across all areas of launch. Some things click, some don't. It's important to isolate what's working, especially things that pertain to consumer likeability, from those that aren't. This is to avoid a general pronouncement of failure and surgically examine and correct things that aren't working. This only works when your ear is close to the ground, and openness and willingness to fix small problems exist.

Secure support: Success requires that all key stakeholders rally behind your product. It's critical therefore to align sales, finance, manufacturing and procurement constantly with sharing of positive success to enlist their inputs for keeping the initial high going. Failure to do so may conversely lead to a fledgling success getting denied the encouraging environment of growth.

Expand success: If there is a thumping success in the first few weeks of launch, one can get lulled into complacency. To avoid that and to continue notching early gains, a better strategy is to expand the early signals of success, so early gains become irreversible. Here, it's important to move with caution. Moving too fast can be deleterious; hence, it's critical that one times it right. The advice of seniors, scenario building and financial capabilities to support an expansion should be considered. Expansion of geography, retail, media support, selling volumes, supplementary SKUs and secondary packaging—these are important to galvanize a system already on a high.

Branch out: Sometimes ideas to support a launch can come after you have put out the product. Don't be shy, don't hesitate. Mount them with purpose and keenness and secure cross-functional support only citing the increasing chance of success with additional initiatives. Setting up a service pillar, feedback desk, consumer engagement cell, digital re-targeting, e-commerce alliances, institutional deals or a topical PR opportunity are the areas to look out for actively.

Initial branching out can make dodgy success a certainty and sometimes even give a dodgy start a strong footing.

Mid-course corrections: A little fix, a change in the marketing mix plan or a redoing of positioning—if you have any such qualms, don't be disheartened. It happens with the best initiatives. Either find a way to refuel your new product mid-air or take a small break, aligning stakeholder expectation, and relaunch quickly. Not only will this win respect from all, especially trade, but also give you a much better chance to succeed when you reappear.

Often corrections may not be made for fear of embarrassing oneself and harming one's career. But not getting it right when solutions were in sight (and you don't want someone else to spot it when you are in command) is equally harmful. The flipside is that your tenacity and sincere commitment to get it right will be appreciated more than if you had a straight-line success.

Innovations are finally tricky. Statistically, very few make it. But they needn't be confined to products alone. We saw in the example above that it can span communication and consumer engagement opportunities as well. Any manager who has made it to the top is usually associated with some innovative initiative or other. Without approaching innovation across all areas of work and consistently so, you are quite unlikely to shine. And sometimes, many small innovations and a relentless pursuit of innovation can do the trick for you, even if one big innovation eludes you.

This is how critical innovation is in imparting you with leadership status, because it fuses the best of strategy with the best of execution skills.

Last Tip

Behaving like Start-ups

Office art: Managing yourself

It's not often that managers look at their well-being, in all respects, as they are submerged into building themselves and their brand. To stay ahead in the brand, however, it's important that you need to be professionally and personally in control of your life. A few watch-outs are important.

It's important to build a practice of evaluating how you are working and feeling. Once a day, take a break (happens naturally to smokers, but not others). This allows the muddle of mounting pressure to settle down, allowing your thinking and composure to show up, naturally. Give yourself the space to combat difficulties or become creative so the situation neither bogs you nor prevents you from thinking differently.

Focus on what matters, let go of what doesn't. Develop the distance to evaluate the impact of your activities on brand building with objectivity and then proceed to stop doing what is wasteful and accelerate what matters. It's important to not do what one likes, but what matters. Often managers can end up chasing a futile cause because they feel a sense of heroism in taking on a daunting task when the returns are rather poor. Energy and time are scarce resources that managers need to deploy judiciously. Recognizing when to quit is as critical as staying doggedly on the task.

Build your support system to counsel you when in doubt or when you are down. Office seniors, mentorship with cross-functional colleagues, or friends with no political agenda can be useful conduits for letting out steam and drawing invigorating ideas. Make an effort to develop cross-linkages where possible and value them. You don't have to be a social gadfly in office knowing everyone, but being comfortable with a few who matter is a time-tested way to endure unprofessional office difficulties.

Finally, keep an eye on personal gain from professional ways. Ask if a certain brand success will help grow your career. Have the conversation with seniors and establish the boundaries of awards and recognition when you start to contribute positively to the company. This is not to advocate a constant self-serving agenda behind professional moves but an enduring awareness of the spin-off of work on your personal life. You don't want to be left behind as others are walking away with credit for a less spectacular performance than you. Personal growth is important for developing your confidence and motivation to contribute to brand management. Otherwise you could lose steam and interest in your brand.

Now, let's jump into the emerging world of business which requires the maximum skills and competencies of brand management: start-ups.

Start-up must-wins

In a sense, start-ups reflect some of the best principles of business: they are dynamic, practical within an evolving theoretical framework and extremely close to Indian consumers. Also, we find that within large multinational companies, the qualities of entrepreneurship are highly valued. But the truth is that while most bosses will want their subordinates to behave like entrepreneurs, they are, in fact, the hurdle, being perpetrators of red tape and elaborate processes that impede the organization's escape velocity from mediocrity.

What do the start-ups do right? We interviewed a few and realized a few abiding traits that set them apart from the usual corporate-dom. First was clarity of vision—they knew exactly where they wanted to be even if they didn't understand all the tricks to get there. Second, they pulled a team of people who would contribute above their weight because resources are scarce and whatever is available has to be maximized. Third, high external awareness: they showed a high degree of knowledge of what was happening in their proximal and distant circle which impacted their business—this is a dual quality, they look out all the time, but they only look as far as is required for their cause. Fourth, flexibility in approach. Since survival is critical in the founding years, they excel in adapting to the outside world for maximizing returns. Finally, indefatigability: the sheer energy levels that they bring to bear at work is much higher than normal employees. So, employees in the company who exhibit these qualities are more likely to be like start-up entrepreneurs than normal people.

There has been a massive proliferation of start-ups in recent times—testimony to the rising tide of innovation in India. It's less than China and the US, but no less significant in terms of its potential impact on the way we do business in India. What is the start-up journey, its challenges and learnings, its travails and bounties?

Start-ups, as per Eric Ries in his book *The Lean Startup*, are human institutions designed to create a new product or service under conditions of extreme uncertainty. After evaluating start-ups across different industrial segments in India, the typical journey of entrepreneurs in this space bears out certain learnings that can be detailed in the following stages:

Figure 12.1

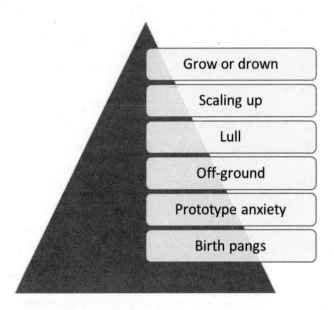

Birth pangs: Entrepreneurs have compelling hallucinations of their ideas at the start. They know they could be disappointed with the pursuit of their idea but, more than that, they know they will be doomed if they don't put it to the test. Do all ideas start as being unique and unheard of? Is absolute novelty the way to judge the worth of the idea? Apparently not. At least, not always. If the idea is too obvious, it's probably taken or easily replicable; if it's too abstract, it may not be real at all. Hence, a worthwhile idea may hang somewhere between familiarity and novelty. This may sound easier said than done, but a few pointers towards a good idea are:

1. There is some elementary evidence of the idea in operation, though rudimentary and incompletely envisaged. It may be as simple as going online with an already prospering offline idea, like online booking for hotels and airlines (Makemytrip), or tutorials (Egurukool), or movie booking (bookmyshow).

2. The idea complements a new emerging technology as a convenient adjacency. With rise of T20, the need for interactive, live cricket updates (cricinfo) or books rating and sharing with the rise of Kindle (Goodreads). Such opportunities are relatively less risky and success can be evaluated by benchmarking the big trend of which this is a part.

3. An idea that is adjacent yet potentially discontinuous due to intermediate layers. Twitter is close to publishing since it's in the public domain with hashtagging, yet it's your personal view which was unheard of till its launch. In this case, the opportunity has to be part imagined, part in evidence, but the risk stays.

4. A new to world idea like Facebook where the insight is human need to connect with near and dear ones but carries the risk of being commercially untested. The result here is either windfall gain due to uniqueness or a complete flop because of its bizarreness.

5. Sometimes an idea is contrary to the prevailing wisdom in that category: For instance, iPod went against the prevailing wisdom of the analogue Walkman that people were willing to download music but they wouldn't pay for it. Jobs proved it was possible if the end product offered limitless storage and unheard-of experiences—an antilog idea that went on to revolutionize the market.

6. At other times, the idea may have to be modified beyond the original design. For instance, Groupon began with the idea of a 'collective activism platform' on things of general interest such as fund-raising for a cause or boycotting a retailer, but Andre Mason, its founder, simplified it to offer coupon deals gauging the public reaction to one of his incidental sub-offers.

Whatever the stage of the idea, most entrepreneurs would confess that they are eventually drawn to trying out their idea without having all the answers at the start. Often this comes at the cost of a more certain pursuit for the risk-taker. Yet they take the plunge, with or without counselling or sufficient capital.

Prototype anxiety: To bring an idea to life, one needs quick prototyping. Whether this is a technology platform or a final product to consumers, or a service in a limited area, what is critical is a shape as good as final so consumer reaction is correctly measured. Eric Ries talks about the need for creating a Minimum Viable Product (MVP) that costs less, is efficiently turned around and represents the basic features of the final product that is envisaged for launch. Getting this right is critical to success: too late and you miss the bus, too early and you misjudge the reaction because of prototype limitations. With the right start, an entrepreneur can get a 'validated learning' that would provide the right signals for future growth.

Zomato started the aggregation of restaurants in a limited area to test the receptivity of consumers to home delivery of a variety of products at a good price, before scaling up. Early signs of success not only allowed them to draw funds but also make mid-course corrections to perfect the model later. At early stages, it's better to think big and start small than to wait for the perfect product or service to get started at all.

Off-ground: As the prototype hits the ground, it's important to make it as real as possible—to stretch it, to test it for endurance and expose it to all uncertainties so that enough learning is attained in the early stages to avoid monumental failures later. The mantra is Build–Measure–Learn in quick and repeated loops rather than the long chain of trying and testing that may put small fixes out of view and make the diagnosis of failures foggy down the line.

A critical attitude during this period is what Toyota usually embraces: Genchi Gembutsu, which means 'Go and see for yourself' where the action is. Successful entrepreneurs show this attitude from the start, willing to roll their sleeves up time and again to fix every nut and bolt of their idea machinery. Big Basket in their founding years spent years fixing warehousing and servicing of highly perishable grocery products till they got the right balance of freshness, variety and minimal wastages. There is no alternative to running the process cog again and again, till through ground-iteration one is able to set the best algorithm for your follow-up team to implement. Also, there is no certainty that once the model template is established, it will survive for long. Being open to demolishing your favourite models is an absolute must in this game of loving what you do, as much as distancing yourself from what you do, every once in a while.

Most start-ups will start to smell rosy or rotten at this stage. It's the first stage that an entrepreneur can start to truly assess the worth of the idea, or even open up to outside venture capitalists or angel investors to visit his model. This stage is very critical for survival or death for most start-ups.

Lull: Most entrepreneurs talk of a stage of lull following early success or failure. This could be due to a variety of reasons, but it's important to decode them closely as unlocking these would herald the next big wave up or spell a downward plunge. Typical reasons that were elicited for a slowdown are:

- Scale as a reason for the model to work. Many models just require the whole process to turn around faster and with more volume to become viable at various ends of the supply chain. Other than that, there is nothing amiss with the model—it's like the engine of a 500 cc bike that only delights above a certain speed when all else is in place. Supply chain models, data aggregation centres and insurance fintech portals are some examples of models where more is better. A thorough scrutiny of process and checking for any other blocks should establish if scale is the only issue and should be addressed appropriately.
- Expertise: A model may require an added feature which is missing to complete the jigsaw, and deliver the required success.

No serious remodelling is required here. An expert's advice or a detailed customer feedback may unlock this opportunity. For instance, adding a chat feature in Momspresso helped trigger mothers' conversations, increasing participation and user-generated content.

-   Appeal limitation: The idea is either very niche or moderately exciting, limited in appeal only to the initial adopters. The option is either to broad-base the appeal or seriously evaluate a closure to relaunch and avoid compounding failures downstream.

This is also the stage at which entrepreneurs have to make the hard decision between what Eric Ries calls Pivot or Persevere. The right decision is crucial to building a wonder or a blunder. Otherwise there is no bigger destroyer of creative potential than the misguided decision to persevere. Pivoting allows one to keep one leg in the current situation but also start making corrections with the other though optimizing, tuning and iterating till the model is fine-tuned. The opportunities for pivot identified by Eric Ries are as follows:

-   Zoom in pivot: A single feature of the product becomes important enough to be the whole product. In spite of many features, Makemytrip won customers mostly on air ticketing.
-   Zoom out pivot: The single feature becomes the base for more services from the same platform as in the expansion to Uber Eats from Uber commuting service.
-   Customer segment/need pivot: When the customers of a product turn out to be different from the ones expected initially, or the need being catered to turns out to be different. For instance, a logistics company turns out to be more suited for IT solutions for a different set of customers, or a dog grooming service turns out to be more appropriate for dog sitting as an alternative need.
-   Business architecture pivot: A business that may have been designed to serve for retail turns out to be more profitable in

the out-of-home segment for a beverage drink. Or a business conceived as low margin, high volume ends up making more sense as high margin, but low volumes.

- Engine of growth pivot: A business may have two primary engines of growth—viral and paid. This decides the extent of the revenue stream and the pace at which it accrues. The business may decide to go slow or fast adjusting with commensurate profit expectations.
- Channel pivot: A business designed for traditional trade ends up working better on e-commerce, or what is designed for e-commerce can be taken into the mass market depending on the quality of response from consumers.
- Technology pivot: In the course of working, a company may discover a more efficient or effective technology and may accordingly fine-tune its product or service design for optimum results. This can happen typically with aggregators who depend more on back-end economics than real marketplace variables.

Scaling up: The initial response is an unequivocal hit and now, to make it attractive, it needs to expand rapidly before the idea is either copied or loses steam because of the entrepreneur's inability to refresh it with fresh and relevant content for the ones who are already converted. Enter the world of angel investors and venture capitalists.

An interesting aspect emerging in India is the difference in the manufacturing design of new companies. Traditionally, scale operations have supported large, standardized manufacturing to reduce costs and delight consumers with defined features that are made desirable by high-octane advertising. However, with mass adoption of technology in India and the increasing power of social media, consumers are expressing themselves widely in real time. A fundamental change of this kind is forcing companies to look at more customized rather than one-size-fits-all kind of designs. The earliest pioneer of this was Toyota, which countered the Henry Ford mass line production in Japan with small batches of production. The internal tooling of automobiles was changed to create fewer, but more distinctive cars, which could be easily modified unlike their inflexible large capital machinery in the West. Also, unlike the West, if a mistake was made in assembling, it could be interrupted mid-way through the 'Andon Cord' (or worker intervention at will) rather than late, mechanistic discovery at the end of the line, concurrent with huge losses.

To an extent, the Indian market is favouring small differentiated designs. The success of Paperboat drinks which stormed the market with a novel format of packaging and new flavours challenged the monolithic landscape of cola players.

For start-ups, the inherent advantage of disrupting the market is best leveraged with small batch size production rather than an inflexible and standardized industrial block of manufacturing that gives consumers no distinctiveness as users. In fact, with advances in 3D printing, the world is moving to individualized pieces of manufacturing and start-ups have a distinct advantage in this space.

Grow or drown: As start-ups mature, they move towards glory or extinction. Since the market is dynamic, a robust growth is when the rate of customer acquisition exceeds the churn rate. From a financial perspective, the cost of acquisition is less than the lifetime value of a customer, when the business is headed northwards.

In the initial phase, word of mouth becomes very critical for registering early growth. When Hotmail was launched, they offered freemail with a click option at the end of their e-mail, which spun off huge growth at a very early stage of launch. Another useful measure of the viral strength of an idea is viral coefficient. The higher the coefficient, the faster the product spreads as it happens with direct selling in Amway where each consumer is a potential seller, multiplying impact on ground multifold even with limited direct contact with the company.

Marc Andreessen, one of the fathers of 'worldwideweb' (www), called this the phenomenon of product/market fit. When the start-up acquires several consumers that resonate with the product, explosive growth occurs, creating a constantly learning and adaptive organization.

However, one can easily misjudge failures as success and the other way around. To segregate a successful performance from a failed one, the principle of five whys has been proposed by Taiichi Ohno of Toyota to get to the root cause of a problem. An example of such an analysis is as follows:

- Why did the machine stop – overload
- Why was there an overload – bearing not lubricated
- Why was the bearing not lubricated – lubrication pump not working right
- Why was it not pumping sufficiently – shaft of the pump was worn out
- Why was the shaft worn out – nobody had attended to it

Hence, at the end, a people fault or system fault was found. A similar exercise can be undertaken in organizations to nail the right reason and prevent the wrong diagnosis from writing off a project. However, for this, a non-blaming culture has to be evolved in the organization, with tolerance for mistakes the first time but not subsequently. This way, unpleasant truths can be faced and acted upon.

Most entrepreneurs agree that the one thing that sets a successful start-up apart from a failed one is the personal investment of the founding father. That not only ensures the right investment at the right place but an excruciating level of attention to detail to plug the most minor hole, while spotting the smallest opportunity.

Who are the right people to support start-ups? No one kind of manager fits the various stages but certain archetypes can be established corresponding to the evolution of the start-up.

- For the initial stage when the new product is getting established, you need innovative marketers.
- Once a certain level of stability is acquired, managers who excel in optimization, delegation, control and execution should be favoured.
- And as operations increase and the bottom line assumes criticality, managers with expertise in outsourcing, automation and cost reduction will be in demand.

Successful entrepreneurs have an uncanny ability to either shift their gears to play different roles at different stages or hire people who exhibit these tendencies. Failing this, good ideas may sink without a trace.

As you grow in brand management, whatever the size of the company, it would be extremely beneficial if you acquire some of the traits of start-up professionals. They are nimble, effective and extremely sharp on consumer focus. In the emerging world, these are qualities you would want to certainly acquire in your life.

Epilogue

Summing up, we have traversed a whole gamut of skills and competencies of brand management. It's time to score yourself again and see how much you have moved up.

Figure 1.3: BQ score grid

Managerial skills	Score (0–10)	Office art	Score (0–10)	Brand competencies	Score (0–10)
Shaper		Boss management		Brand knowledge	
Team worker		Making an early impact		Consumer need	
Researcher		Understanding company culture		Knowing the consumer	
Improviser		Effective cross-alliances		Segmentation and targeting	
Visionary		Checking tendency bias		Positioning	
Executor		Building teams		Communication	
Specialist		Managing yourself		Cult brand	

Managerial skills	Score (0–10)	Office art	Score (0–10)	Brand competencies	Score (0–10)
				Integrated marketing	
				Innovation	
Total					
Grand Total					

Three options could emerge from the above:

- Less than 150: Revise some of the fundamentals and revisit them in real life.
- Between 150 and 200: You have understood the principles and started applying them too. Keep going, you can only get better.
- More than 200: Celebrate. You will go far, maybe even make history, provided you stay grounded.

How many brand managers want to leave a legacy? Most probably, all. And why not? Making brands is a job with creative satisfaction not very different from other creative arts: painting, music and films. Something gets created which didn't exist before, it gives others a better experience and gives your pursuit some meaning. Aren't these motivations for art and brand management equal? Brand management is a lot like art and for that reason, it does attract people with a lateral bent or those who are fired off by the tremendous possibilities of creating something new, no matter how difficult the road.

Taking this argument further, we know that where there is art there is an artist. Likewise, where there is a brand there is a brand manager. Authorship of art is a critical driver for artists who seek fame through it. Brand managers also want to see their creativity and hard work recognized. It's therefore, very common amongst superlative brand managers to seek personal glory in building their brands. It's in fact a powerful source of motivation and sees them through many trammels and mundanities of this job. So, we can conclude it's desirable for brand managers to put their name next to the brand.

However, brands are owned by companies and consumers in the final analysis. Also, the job requires a great amount of team work with equal participation from all, which stands in sharp contrast to an individual's need for self-glorification over others. How do you reconcile these?

There is no easy answer to this contradiction. But both are important: a high personal involvement in brand management to lead it creatively like your own canvas, as also extreme team orientation to manage its multiple interface within and outside businesses. Managers have to develop both capabilities even if they seem contrarian.

Over time, surprisingly, a balance of both does emerge. You can create a great brand or you can lead a great team that develops it. Somewhere in the course of brand management the two become synonymous and taking credit becomes as easy as sharing or showering it. How that happens is another paradox but it happens. It may have to do with the fact that brand management is as much outward looking at consumers, as inward looking for the brand managers who have to access their deepest lateral and analytical skills to make a difference.

And the results of successful brand development are countless. Consumers are delighted, stakeholders relish the increasing returns, and society benefits if various brands move towards enhancing the lives of people as they go about their lives. You only have to look at a developed country against a developing world to realize how deeply brands have contributed to making life less punishing and tedious, freeing time for more satisfactory pursuits in life.

Yes, brands have a big role in bringing a smile to your consumer's face. Think for a moment not as a brand manager but as a consumer. Your happiness may be vaguely attributable to the right toothpaste in the morning, to the best fabric that you wore to work, driving that sporty car that reflects your personality; but by the evening when you are eating in your restaurant with your preferred brand of wine, you realize that you are very much a happy recipient of brand offerings. So many brands contribute to making a full life that the impact of any one may not be seen till you aggregate them. Now, compare that with a poor farmer in the village doing his daily chores without the benefit of all the luxuries that brands have brought to your door and you can see what a phenomenal difference brands make.

Brand management and brand managers should invoke this vision to fire themselves and others for improving value to consumers in every transaction. It's a priceless way to drive purpose in one and all in the organization.

As we march into the next decade, the winners of this game will be those brands that not only delight consumers but do so sustainably. Cause marketing or responsible marketing is a critical input to future-ready your brands. From sourcing to packaging to delivery systems to waste disposal, the whole spectrum of the brand journey needs to be laid bare for transparency and systematically improved with consumers' co-participation. Brands began in the manufacturers' stable in Europe a couple of centuries ago. The opportunity for brands to be invited into the consumer's living room is emerging ever so often.

Brand managers who realize the future trajectory of brands will make their job bigger than it is today and co-create with their consumers a brand experience more enriching than ever before.

Those who fail to recognize and join this forward march of brands will have to be content just watching it, not shaping it.

Raise your BQ, shape the change and lead unequivocally with the brandvantage. All the best.

End